THE 51 FATAL
BUSINESS ERRORS
AND HOW TO AVOID THEM

JIM MUEHLHAUSEN, CPA, JD

PUBLISHING

Second Edition, 2008

Copyright © 2003–2008 by Jim Muehlhausen
and Maxum Communications, Inc.

Illustrations by Digital Heroes
Cover and book design: 1106 Design

Published by
Maxum Communications, Inc.
9465 Counselors Row, Suite 200
Indianapolis, IN 46240

Orders: 877-903-6287

www.51errors.com

Printed and bound in the U.S.A.

ISBN: 978-0-9816082-0-4

41935320   10/09

DEDICATION

This book is dedicated to my wife, Beth, and my children, Rachel and Hannah. The book is also dedicated to the many business owners I have had the pleasure to work with. Without their openness, candor and dedication to their craft, this book would not be possible.

Special thanks to Marla Eurick, who pushed me into putting pen to paper. Andy Cleary and Ed Gill were instrumental in making several points in the book clearer. Many thanks to all of the CEO Focus facilitators for their stories, intellect and support during this process.

Most importantly, thanks to you, the reader. Unlike many books in the genre, this one does not offer easy fixes, nor is it meant to be a rah-rah to puff you up and blow smoke at you. In fact, this book will require a sometimes painful look in the mirror to help you improve your business practices. Kudos to you for having the fortitude to spend time working on the most important parts of your business.

Here's to growing your business!

—Jim Muehlhausen

DISCLAIMER

The advice contained in this book might not be suitable for everyone. The author designed the information to present his opinion about the subject matter, and the reader should carefully investigate every aspect of any business decision before committing him or herself. The author obtained the information contained in this book from sources he deems reliable, or from personal experience, but he neither implies nor intends any guarantee of accuracy. The author is not in the business of giving legal, accounting, or any other professional advice. Should the reader need such advice, he or she should seek out a competent professional. The author particularly disclaims any liability, loss, or risk taken by individuals who directly or indirectly act on the information contained in this book or that is on the associated website: *www.51errors.com*. The author believes the advice presented in this book is sound, but he cannot be held responsible for readers' actions nor the results of those actions.

CONTENTS

FOREWORD

As a business advisor—our firm specializes in building brands for growing businesses—I admit that I inhaled the first edition of *The 51 Fatal Errors — and How to Avoid Them* like a J.K. Rowling fan devouring the latest Harry Potter potboiler. It was lucky I started reading on Friday night so I didn't have to miss work.

In *51 Fatal Errors* (my nickname for the book), I saw many of my own customers, vendors and associates reflected in its pages. Of course I also saw myself as a business owner of 24 years. It was fun to observe several errors that were near misses, some that hit me square in the forehead that I was lucky to survive and some that I might presently be in the process of committing. Most business owners need a copy of *51 Fatal Errors* delivered to their door overnight with several chapter titles kindly circled in red.

Eventually I was fortunate enough to meet Jim Muehlhausen in the context of his organization, CEO Focus. Our first conversation went something like this:

    Me: Jim, I'm glad to make your acquaintance
            by phone. We have a mutual friend and I've
            heard nothing but the best about you.

    Jim: Now Andy, if we're to have some sort of business rela-
            tionship, the way I work is straight shooting right out
            of the box. You will not be blowing smoke up mine and

I will not blow smoke up yours—we've got to be frank
with each other or this is definitely not going to work.

Me: I can appreciate that Jim, but honestly, I *have* heard good
things about you.

Jim: Alright then. Let's start.

So I instantly took a liking to the Jim Muehlhausen brand of business. As I found out more about him—his background in accounting (CPA), law (JD), family business, franchise ownership, small business ownership and founding of a nationwide CEO board organization—I discovered his breadth of experience is matched by his passion for understanding business trends.

Jim speaks fluent business-ese. If you mention a business concept, he not only has read the book but has a unique "take" on it. When he gets going on a topic, he speaks business shorthand expecting you to keep up as he rumbles like a train to his point. And every conversation has a point.

Jim is definitely iconoclastic in spirit. He loves to smash all those comforting little self-defeating and false-justification tapes that we business owners play in our heads. He doesn't like to waste time, although he recognizes the need for it. He doesn't judge you, but will give you a good stiff "mule kick" just when you need it. His "Jimisms" are hard knocks delivered with candor and laconic bits of business wisdom. I once asked him why he got into the CEO peer board business. He said "Because it works; when I look at your business I'm a genius. When I look at my own business, I'm an idiot."

With the breadth of his background and education, Jim could have an extreme case of "been there, done that," but Jim is down to earth in advising his CEO crowd. He always operates with an air of what I call "respectful disrespect"—he may give you a mule kick or two but you realize that by virtue of being a business owner you've "got game" and always have Jim's utmost respect.

You will find that *The 51 Fatal Business Errors — and How to Avoid Them* is a good place to learn and laugh at what goes horribly awry in business and a chance to learn and laugh at yourself.

So that is my introduction to the book and the phenomenon that is Jim Muehlhausen. I didn't blow any smoke up yours so please do not blow any smoke up mine.

—Andy Cleary, President
Orbit Design
Genius Simple Branding

INTRODUCTION

Using the Gym Membership

For more than twenty-five years, I have watched entrepreneurs, myself included, learn about the business world the only way they knew how: from the School of Hard Knocks. Let's face it, business is not learned in school and those with brand new MBAs are not truly equipped for success. Business is learned by doing, indeed from the School of Hard Knocks. The frustrating part is that the School of Hard Knocks is expensive and one's progress through the program is slow. Entrepreneurial CEOs have no patience for either the expense or waiting. Consequently, I wrote *The 51 Fatal Business Errors* to help you learn some of the lessons from the School of Hard Knocks more quickly by offering my own hard-earned knowledge (in fact, I have several advanced degrees from that illustrious institution).

Most business books are like gym memberships: lots of initial enthusiasm and not much meaningful action. These books are great in theory, but any theory is useless unless put into practice. We all "know" we need to exercise, and we all know we need to revise our business procedures. I do not want to be another business writer selling you on the business equivalent of the benefits of a health club membership. Done wrong, a business book is nothing more than theoretical generalities that get you "juiced up" but have no real impact on you or your business. Done right, a business book should energize you AND leave you with tangible action items to make your business better.

This book is not about whether or not to go to the health club, but what to DO when you walk in the door. I want to move past the **temporary excitement** of a new idea and into **permanent gain** created by making meaningful, lasting changes. My goal in this book is to give you specific tools for using "the gym equipment," thereby empowering you to get your business in good shape. I want to energize you about your business's boundless possibilities while giving you practical action steps to move your business to the next level. This book is designed to be used as a reference that you can come back to repeatedly as new issues arise in your business that need "toning."

As you can probably guess, with a name like Muehlhausen, my nickname as a kid was "Mule." In my current career as a business coach and writer, I found myself giving clients a kick in the butt to make a point. Combine the two, and you have a Mule-kick, which is my gift to you: a harsh lesson in reality that will help you improve your business. I will give you many Mule-kicks in this book, but I don't give a Mule-kick out of mean-spiritedness, ego, or as a joke. I will give you a Mule-kick out of compassion, empathy (been-there, done-that), and the desire to see you succeed. Watching a CEO fall short of their full potential is far "meaner" than giving them a Mule-kick. A Mule-kick is designed to give you the little jolt you need to change your mode of operation or perspective, or simply to do that uncomfortable task.

When you see   I am giving you a Mule-kick!

Each individual error discussed in this book is divided into sections that highlight a problem area. The first section is a description of the "error," which is followed by a real-life example (and all of the stories in this book are real-life examples) and a concrete solution. Many of the errors contain a bonus available as a free download on my website. The names and circumstances in the book have been changed for illustration purposes.

CHAPTER 1

Enter
at Your Own Risk

C aution: this book is not for the faint at heart or those who are overly satisfied with their current business results. I wrote this book for the select few entrepreneurs who are serious about taking meaningful action in their business. The world is full of business people who talk about what they need to do, but the real professionals actually do something about it. This book is premised upon that paradigm, which means it is quite possible that parts of the book will actually tick you off. When you find yourself annoyed with me, and it will happen, please keep reading. There are hundreds of points and observations in this book. You don't have to agree with all of them.

My goal is to challenge your thinking, not to throw platitudes at you. In fact, there will be some points in this book with which you completely disagree. Disagreement is not an issue in and of itself. Many of the points in the book are my subjective opinion, but they are based on years of case studies and personal experience. In fact, every point in this book may cause you to be uncomfortable. Before discounting the points, I challenge you to consider each of them in turn and recognize the nuggets that are applicable to your life or business. However, do not discount the points with which you are uncomfortable without first asking yourself why it makes you uncomfortable. Could it be that your discomfort is caused by a real belief that the point is not true or applicable, or, in fact, does it really apply and hit too close to home?

Warning #1: I will get in your face a bit. My style is to challenge you, which is a style that works well for me in the coaching world. As a professional business coach, it is my job to ask you tough, probing questions that make you REALLY think. More importantly, it is my job to ask questions that make you act. Moving this very personal style over to an impersonal book is difficult because you cannot see my expressions and overall demeanor. I promise that my tough questions are an act of compassion, and so that style may not translate perfectly to a book. Consequently, I want to remind you that I will challenge you and that I will get in your face, because I want your business to be GREAT. Every CEO I have met has the talent and capability to drive their business to great heights. However, many of them are falling short of their true potential. Let's work together to take your business to that next level of greatness.

Warning #2: I use the phrase "small business." I am a small businessman, and most likely, so are you. I have been told that some people get offended by the word "small," but small means merely "non-big." I like Uncle Sam's definition of a small business. The SBA defines a small business as less than fifty million dollars in sales and fewer than five hundred employees. To my mind, a fifty million dollar company is a nice enterprise, and maybe that is something for all "small" business to aim for.

If you are serious about taking your business to the next level, then let's get to work.

CHAPTER 2

What's Good for G.E. Isn't Always Good for G.E.

Alright, I owe you an explanation for the title of this chapter. The real title is "What's Good for General Electric Isn't Always Good for Gus's Electric." Most of the business press coverage is written for or about large businesses like General Electric, and significant coverage of a business issue becomes conventional wisdom. Closely-held businesses cannot always follow the same wisdom, however. I refer to the instances when the conventional wisdom doesn't fit a Myth-Buster.

If you are familiar with the term "thinking outside the box," then you understand 10% of the value of a myth-buster. A myth-buster is also innovative, creative, and dynamic. One of the biggest problems with conventional wisdom is that it is PAST TENSE. It WAS wisdom, a static assertion. You have to decide if a business assertion is still wisdom, whether it fits your business, and most importantly, whether that business assertion will continue to be wise in the future. True wisdom is specific to your business and is fluid. The timeline below illustrates my point.

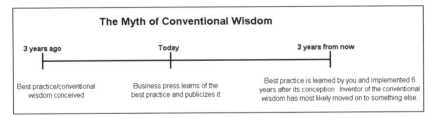

In the 1960s, the conventional wisdom was to create conglomerates of diverse companies with no common thread. Bigger was better. Today, this conventional wisdom has been thrown out in favor of highly focused smaller companies that can dominate a category.

In the 1970s, conventional wisdom at automotive companies dictated a supervisor-to-employee span of control of around 1 to 10. Employees were deemed to be less productive if they were not tightly supervised. The Japanese challenged this conventional wisdom with a highly empowered workforce and a span of control of around 1 to 50. This strategy proved a competitive advantage for the Japanese until U.S. automakers adopted a similar strategy.

Some of the best business ideas challenge the conventional wisdom, but again, a myth-buster goes beyond thinking outside the box. A myth-buster challenges the typical modus operandi and combines it with a creative solution. Imagine the grief the inventors of the ATM must have endured. They must have heard, "Who would want to bank with a robot instead of a human?" Conventional wisdom becomes conventional wisdom typically because it is wise AT THE TIME. However, wisdom is fluid and can also be specific to your business or to a given business situation. You must be willing to challenge the world's conventional wisdom but also your own accepted wisdom. The discussion of the following errors is meant to jumpstart your ability to challenge convention.

Fatal Error #1:
Hiring Your Competitor's Rejects

If you hire "experienced" people, you are really hiring your competitor's rejects. I know, you don't believe me, but I can prove it. Every CEO wants to hire the perfectly qualified person for a given position, which typically means the employee has done the job before, for someone else — the competition. When you hire the "perfect person" from the competition, however, you are hiring a reject. Here is why. If you are a chemical distributor needing an accounts payable person with SAP experience, whom do you want to hire? Someone with chemical industry experience, accounts payable experience, and SAP experience, right? It seems perfectly logical. This is really a recipe for disaster.

This strategy is a disaster because you are making an incorrect assumption, that your competitor will let a truly great employee leave. Picture this: Sally is your ten-year tenured payables clerk. She is truly a great employee. The department would fall apart without Sally. One day, Sally walks into your office and says,

> *Mr. CEO, I love working here. You are the best boss I could ever ask for. I always figured I would retire from here. I don't want you to take this as a shakedown, but ABC Company offered me a job for $1.50 more per hour. Normally, I would have said no, but my boy is sick and we really need the money. I just wanted to say thanks for everything you have done and let you know I will be leaving in two weeks.*

What would you do? Most people would pay Sally $1.50 more per hour rather than have their payables department fall apart. You lose a lot if you lose Sally. You lose ten years of experience and competence. You lose ten years of training. You lose Sally's relationship with your vendors/customers. So what do you do? You hang on to Sally for dear life! Guess what, **SO WOULD YOUR COMPETITORS!** You are deluded if you believe the person you are interviewing is one of these great employees. The fact that the employee is sitting in front of you means that the "please don't leave, Sally!" conversation did **NOT** happen with their boss. Therefore, you are talking to someone the competitor did **NOT** try to keep (a reject, plain and simple).

I realize there are exceptions to my story. Everyone has had one: a failed business owner, a competitor going out of business, a competitor's cash flow issues that preclude giving anyone a raise, etc. I will take all of the truly indispensable employees I can get from my competitors' bad luck or bad choices. However, these circumstances are the exception, not the rule. Pretending these anomalies will repeat over and over is not a good plan.

Are you using your gut instinct to hire because you have faith in yourself, or because you are being lazy? I will give you the benefit of the doubt and say it is because you have confidence in your instincts. Either way, however, you can trust your gut but trust your testing methods MORE.

There is an old saying: "Every employee looks like a movie star on paper." Many potential employees are better at interviewing than they are at performing the job. As far as I can tell, the ability to puff up a resume or to talk well during an interview has little to do with FUTURE job performance.

CAVEAT

Occasionally it makes sense to go outside the company for a high-level person of specific talent, particularly if a company is growing.

Employment growth may exceed a company's ability to grow talent, which creates a need to buy talent. However, if you do buy talent, be prepared to pay well or you will surely be hiring a reject. You should stick to the "hire aptitude" plan for entry-level people.

REAL-LIFE EXAMPLE

Tom had an awful time hiring quality customer service personnel. He could only pay $8 an hour and remain profitable, and therefore, he was forced to pull from a workforce with marginal skills. Eventually, Tom realized that hiring people with experience was simply hiring the rejects of his competitors. Instead, Tom focused on hiring people with aptitude for customer service and teaching them the specifics of his business. Tom used a Customer Service Aptitude Test in combination with a computer skills test designed by his current staff. Tom now says that his staff is the best ever, and because he can hire fewer experienced people, Tom's average wage per employee is $0.38 per hour less than before adopting this strategy.

SOLUTION

I firmly believe that you should completely give up on the hope of hiring experienced people and start with inexperienced, high-aptitude employees instead. Once you have identified the high-aptitude people, train them to handle the specifics of your business. Aptitude is discovered by testing, so stop using your gut to hire. It is not that accurate.

Every business has positions where pre-employment testing could result in better hires, but the appropriate personnel at many businesses do not even realize that an abundance of testing mechanisms already exist. I constantly hear the complaint that this person is sloppy or not detail-oriented, but the issue is easily avoided by giving a secretarial skills test to all applicants. This test yields virtually zero percent false positives because a sloppy person simply cannot pass the test. Therefore, bad candidates never qualify for the position and you never have an employee who makes a mess of things.

Personality profiling, such as DISC or Meyer's-Briggs, can help you weed out people who would have a difficult time succeeding in certain positions. Additionally, drug testing is perfectly acceptable in most work environments. Drug-free employees tend to be much more trustworthy and dependable. If you cannot find a ready-made aptitude test, create one yourself. Think of the skills and traits needed to perform well on the job, and create a test accordingly.

Testing provides an adjunct for your own judgment or sensibilities, giving you hard data upon which to base a hiring decision. Testing also identifies the appropriate training that candidates may need to be successful, and testing allows for specific placement in the type of work assigned at a much faster rate, which lowers the cost of your training.

Here are some examples of the types of tests you might consider with specific examples:

- Detail oriented: DISC or Secretarial Skills Test
- Salesmanship: There are a wide variety of tests to measure sales ability. Tests range in cost from $10 to $250 each
- Customer service abilities: Customer service online tests
- Computer skills: Online testing services that test general skills or specific program skills
- Assembly skill: Mechanical aptitude tests or assembly tests

BONUS

Visit *www.51errors.com/reject.html* for DISC links as well as sources for online assessments. If you are looking to truly create a systematic hiring process, check out *www.faqdesigner.com.*

I frequently ask CEOs, "How many of your best employees did you steal from the competition?" The answer is always "none." The bottom line is that most, if not all, of your superstars came via the tried-and-true method of the "cream rising to the top." Hard-working people with high degrees of aptitude rise to the top. Hire such applicants, not your competitors' rejects, and then train the daylights out of them so the cream can rise even faster. The "cream" of your current employees probably rose in spite of your lack of training. Imagine how fast the cream can rise WITH training.

Fatal Error #2:
Revolving Door Policies

As the cartoon below illustrates, sometimes an open door turns into a revolving door. Employees are constantly bustling to get input from the boss. Open door policies were designed for big businesses that need a strategy to break through communication barriers. Small businesses don't have those barriers. The only thing an open door policy does is upset the chain of command and take time away from the most important resource in the company — YOU! Every CEO out there is a bottleneck for their business. This jam is caused in two ways. First, your time and talents and their scarcity (that is, you are the only one with said talents) acts as the "brakes" for your company, slowing the company down when you wish to speed up. An open door policy trades your precious time even-up for a sub-

"The Benefits of Open Door Policies"

ordinate's time, which is a horrible trade in most instances. Second, providing an end-around for people who are struggling with their direct supervisor will cause everything to be dealt with at least twice, and probably more than that. Your time and that of your people is the only asset that you can never replace, so make sure you are making the best use of it. It is a good idea to note that people who make your office door a revolving door are a sign of deeper troubles, and it probably lies within themselves.

Open door policies can also confuse your employees by subverting the chain of command. You would be far better off running your business like the military than non-hierarchically. Major Smith would never think of walking into General Jones' office with an issue. He is forced to work it out with Colonel Johnson. Running your business without a clear chain of command makes each and every employee work less efficiently. By having an open door policy, you are encouraging your employees to break the chain of command as well as allowing them to suck you into minor problems that are not your highest impact activity.

Small business typically runs like a chaotic fire-drill anyway. Things are somewhat unorganized, undermanned, and chaotic. An open door policy only reinforces this dynamic.

REAL-LIFE EXAMPLE

Alan prided himself on his interpersonal skills. He knew the hobbies, kids' and spouses' names, and the personal histories of all thirty of his employees. Alan also prided himself on his open door policy.

His policy worked well for a while because he was exposed to information he would have never heard through regular channels. However, over time, Alan's people took advantage of the policy and stopped their work to enter his office, plop down in a chair, and complain about co-workers or how much they were paid. The last straw was when Alan had an important presentation and could not get a minute to himself. Employees kept interrupting him with issues that were important to them but not important to Alan or the company. Alan's high impact activity, the presentation, was adversely affected by the constant interruptions created by Alan's open door.

SOLUTION

Small businesses need to become MORE structured, not less. The inherent problem with an open door policy is that it creates a permanent mechanism for a business to be unstructured. Worse, gossip is encouraged and rewarded, and employees now have a direct line to the top to demand raises and other concessions. The loss of communication created by a closed-door policy, a policy which admittedly could reduce communication, is far outweighed by the increase in structure and the efficiency of business processes.

Shut your door, but when you do shut it, find a method to get the same important feedback you probably received with your open door policy (along with all the dreck). Set meetings with your key people once a week, or perhaps schedule a specific open door time during the week but disallow gossip or pay demands and insist these meetings are for priority issues that affect the business.

Part of you likes being "in the middle" of everything, right? We entrepreneurs are adrenalin junkies. We enjoy the fast-paced environment of ten different issues coming at us. Here is the problem: if you are doing something reactionary, it is almost ALWAYS low impact. Ask yourself, "One year from now, how will doing this task have moved my business forward?" If it is just a task, we both know the answer: "It won't!"

Fatal Error #3:
Failure to Act Like
a Benevolent Dictator

Miriam Webster defines benevolent as "marked by or disposed to doing good,"[1] and Webster's defines dictator as "one holding complete autocratic control."[2] An autocrat does not have to be a jerk, and a business is not a democracy. Getting employees to "buy-in" is nice, but if they don't, what do you do? You run your business in a kind, democratic, and fair fashion, but if that doesn't work, and on occasion IT WON'T, you need to be a dictator. Please be a benevolent dictator, but be a dictator when needed.

Managing employees is a lot like parenting. Employees may not like what you do, but you have to do it anyway. Many CEOs are afraid to be authoritarian to any extent, even a little, but I will take an authoritarian leader over a democratic one any day. Just because you are authoritarian does not mean you cannot be nice. Remember, it is your name on the door.

REAL-LIFE EXAMPLE

Levi was the third generation to run the family business. The business systems and structure were created long before he was born. Levi's task was to lead the business into the future by leveraging the work that was already done. Like any established business, Levi's business had key personnel, but unfortunately, they disagreed about the future direction of the business. In their weekly meetings, nothing was accomplished beyond arguing, infighting and nitpicking. Levi seemed more concerned with "everyone getting along" than getting things done. He was encouraged to develop a clear vision of where

---

1 Miriam Webster's Online Dictionary. www.m-w.com/dictionary/benevolent
2 www.m-w.com/dictionary/dictator

HE (not everyone else) wanted to take the company. To his credit, he did precisely that, and not surprisingly, everything improved. Once someone was "steering the ship," the infighting stopped because there was nothing to fight about. Business improved, and everyone's job security and pay increased.

SOLUTION

Business is no place for a democracy. I advocate that CEOs run their business as a "benevolent dictator" rather than a democracy. As CEO, you may not be liked, but it is your responsibility to steer the ship and be the commander.

There is no perfect way to run a company, not yours or mine. However, we all have personality characteristics that get in the way of running our company well. Ask yourself, "Do I run my company democratically because I am afraid of conflict?" Can you honestly say that you ENJOY all your key people having a vote on every issue? Aren't there times that you just want to tell them to shut up and do what you say? If so, you ARE letting your personal style get in the way of being the best CEO you can be. Being a CEO is not you, but you filling a role — you playing a part in a play entitled "Joe Jones runs Company X." Play the role the best you can with total disregard to your personal style, preferences or discomfort. You'll thank me later.

Fatal Error #4:
Too Few Meetings

Yes, I said too FEW meetings, which can be a problem for small businesses. The business press line that "meetings are bad…" was written for big business because larger enterprises are notorious for unproductive meetings. Small business owners run their enterprises by the seat of their pants, a practice Steven Covey calls the urgent quadrants. Having a succinct meeting weekly keeps you in the "Not Urgent but Important Quadrant." You can simply call the issues covered in such a meeting "high impact."

Too many CEOs are lousy at keeping a meeting short and to the point, and therefore, meetings become a waste of time because the time-to-accomplishment ratio is out of kilter. Therefore, the CEO feels that the meeting itself is the culprit rather than the CEO's inability to run the meeting.

REAL-LIFE EXAMPLE

Zee's gunslinging management style was perhaps her best entrepreneurial trait. Zee was a master at decisive action, which served her well in the start-up stage, when she could still touch all aspects of the business. She had a small team of loyal followers, but as the business matured, Zee's ability to deal with all aspects of her business diminished. Zee became frustrated with the "poor communication" and "poor morale." It is hard to believe poor morale can be caused by too few meetings, but it was the case. Zee rectified the problem with a one-hour meeting each Friday afternoon, which allowed key management to get on the same page quickly as well as cut off problems in the early stages.

SOLUTION

Have at least one meeting per week and set an agenda for the meeting. Publish that agenda in advance. Set a time for the meeting. Tell all the attendees the time limit for the meeting. This will create pressure on everyone to be succinct. End the meeting at the specified time, even if there are unfinished items, to demonstrate to everyone that you are serious about keeping the meeting brief. If you need a crutch, hold your meetings at the end of the day. For instance, start a one-hour meeting at 4:00 p.m. on a Friday. This should guarantee the meeting will end at 5:00 p.m.

Get creative. Any idiot can hold a four-hour meeting. It takes a genius to accomplish the same amount in one hour. Here are some creative ideas for successful, succinct meetings:

- Getting people to show up on time
    —Impose a small fine that goes into an office pool.
    —Make them sing a tune if they are late.
    —Lock the door one minute after start time.
- Cell phones and email interruptions
    —Have everyone throw their cell phones in a box on the way into the meeting.
    —If someone has an important call, make them announce the potential incoming call, its nature and importance at the beginning of the meeting.
- Ending on time and moving briskly throughout the meeting
    —Have the guts to walk out at the scheduled end time. After a couple of items at the end of the agenda are missed, attendees will get the message.

Fatal Error #5:
Treating Exceptions as the Rule

Everyone is familiar with managing by exception. Managing by exception is Management 101, right? But does managing by exception mean we only manage the exceptions? Some CEOs treat every anomaly as an emergency needing its due attention. Simply because an employee ate bad sushi, got sick all over a client's suit, caused the client to hit his head and then sue you, does not mean we need to create a policy regarding what is suitable to eat at lunch or otherwise spend much time on the situation. After carefully examining a given situation and determining that indeed it is an "isolated" exception, proactively manage the situation by choosing to do absolutely NOTHING about it.

REAL-LIFE EXAMPLE

Bruce had found the perfect employee. Her experience and talent exceeded even Bruce's high standards. Having seen the benefits of a highly talented employee, Bruce began to mentally catalog all the traits of his prize person and ran several ads to find his prize employee's clone. However, Bruce failed to consider that his prize employee moved to town several years ago from California to care for her sick mother. When her mother passed away, she started a job search and found Bruce. Prior to this, she owned a company in the same industry. Bruce's perfect model was a fluke and could not be easily duplicated. Unless Bruce could find a way to convince competitors to sell their business and come to work for him, he was out of luck.

SOLUTION

Learn to recognize and then ignore the true exceptions. In this example, Bruce learned that prior business ownership was helpful but not a model he could duplicate when looking for employees. His prize employee was the exception, not the rule.

The best managers I have seen know the art of "uh huh, uh huh, ignore it." Every business owner has had an employee who feels compelled to plop themselves in a chair and bitch about some meaningless anomaly. The employee only occasionally engages in such behavior, so it certainly isn't actionable. Not only is firing them not an option, but neither is disciplining them or even having a "please stop it" conversation. So what do you do? You politely nod your head, pretend you give a hoot, and forget it ten seconds later (a.k.a.: uh huh, uh huh, ignore it). Don't be ashamed of employing this tactic. It can be excellent management. In fact, not using "uh huh, uh huh, ignore it" when appropriate is bad management.

NOTES:

_____

_____

_____

_____

Fatal Error #6:
Adhering to Unwritten Rules

In Peter Singe's book *The Fifth Discipline*,[3] he calls adhering to unwritten rules a form of systems thinking. Every one of us goes through an unconscious decision-making process, and many times, this process leads to very bad decisions. A common example is industry standards. Industry standards create "conventional wisdom." Remember, sometimes conventional wisdom isn't all that wise! It sounds like this: "Everyone knows you can't do XYZ in the real estate business." However, a smart competitor may come along and challenge this assumption. For instance, look at the turmoil the internet and discount brokers brought to the real estate business. Their fresh perspective created chaos for the rest of the industry.

REAL-LIFE EXAMPLE

Everyone knew the only way to staff a hamburger joint full of $7.00 an hour jobs was to hire sixteen-year-olds. What adult would work for $7.00 an hour? In the 1980s, McDonalds faced a critical labor shortage as American families became wealthier. Teenagers no longer needed to work, so McDonalds was forced to think outside the box. Typical logic dictated that only the economically disadvantaged would work for this wage: the young and the working poor. McDonalds could have filled the vacancies by raising hourly rates, offering recruiting bonuses, or offering college scholarships as the Army did.

Instead, McDonalds found a dependable and inexpensive workforce in the retired. Most of these retirees did not need money, but rather, they were motivated by the opportunity to keep busy and earn additional spending money.

---

3 Senge, Peter M. *The Fifth Discipline: The Art and Practice of the Learning Organization.* (New York: Doubleday, 2006), pp. 6–8.

SOLUTION

Learn to recognize when others are working by "unwritten rules." A friend of mine's wife insists he be home for dinner at 5:30. When I pressed her for an explanation, she did not have an answer. Her demand was simply a want, not a need. However, she was more than willing to turn her family's life upside down to have dinner promptly at 5:30 every day of the year. Once you can identify others "doing it," you can start to see yourself doing it.

There are two types of unwritten rules. The example above is an unwritten rule of convenience. My friend's wife simply did not want to mess with a flexible dinner schedule, so she created an unwritten rule. The other type of unwritten rule is the convention. These rules are typically industry specific, the "everyone in the plastics business knows..." rules.

For instance, think back to the way a grocery store operated in the 1970s. Back then, here is what it took for me to buy a can of beans:

- A stockperson labeled each can of beans "69¢"
- Some person placed each can on the shelf
- When I checked out, the cashier read the can and discovered "69¢" was the price
- The cashier manually punched "69¢" into the cash register
- In the middle of the night, a stockperson eyeballed the shelf and saw the need for more beans
- The stockperson grabbed a piece of paper and wrote an order to the bean company for more beans
- The bean order came in and we started over

This is what is involved in my purchase of a can of beans today:

- I self-checkout and scan the can of beans myself. The machine knows the pricing table from the barcode already on the can. Inventory is adjusted at the time of checkout. Vendors are fed data on stock levels so orders are automatically processed based on actual sales.

If the grocery industry accepted the convention that the old-fashioned "bean system" was the only way of doing business, they would be in trouble.

Learn to be a bit contrarian and don't just accept unwritten rules blindly. Be like a three-year-old and ask "why?"

Another potential cause of unwritten rules is what I call "intellectual bundling." Intellectual bundling is when we take several variables and treat them as if they were one. For instance, a client was struggling with a salesperson getting enough appointments. In this particular business, the salesperson had to push their way in front of the prospect. No one was begging to see them. The salesperson was a detail-oriented person who only felt comfortable if all the details were covered. The sales manager's view was "details kill, just get the appointment and pound out the details later."

In the sales manager's mind, there were several steps in the appointment setting process:

1. Is the prospect willing to take 10 minutes to meet with us under ANY set of circumstances?
2. What is the time of the appointment?
3. What is the length of the appointment?
4. Where is the appointment (at the client location, off-site, etc.)?
5. Is the appointment on the phone or face-to-face?

In the mind of the salesperson, these were all just ONE item. These were the details of getting the appointment, but not separate items. Therefore the salesperson's pitch sounded something like this:

"Hi Bill. This is Joe from ABC. I would like to come by at 3:35 p.m. next Friday to meet you in your office. I know you wanted to meet with our technical engineer, but he won't be available. The appointment is scheduled to last 10 minutes, but many times it lasts up to 30 minutes. Therefore, I want to make sure you have allotted 30 minutes for the call."

In a sales situation, bundling details typically leads to problems. When you are analyzing a situation, challenge yourself to break it down into the tiniest of pieces. Ask yourself, "Is this one variable or two?" Many times, breaking problems down into bite-sized pieces will open up a new solution to the problem.

NOTES:

_____

_____

_____

_____

_____

_____

_____

_____

Fatal Error #7:
Peacock Management

Let's face it, CEOs are problem-solvers by nature. The buck stops with us! We learn very early in our tenure to solve problems. In fact, we learn so well that we learn there is no problem we cannot solve. Have you had an issue in the past year that you did not immediately know the solution? Having solutions to problems is great; however, during this cycle of quickly solving all problems, we train ourselves to believe that "there is no problem I cannot solve."

A quick from-the-hip solution based upon one person's experiences and opinions is rarely the optimal solution, but simply just "a" solution. For instance, I can solve the high cost of gasoline problem by prohibiting automobiles. Demand would fall and so would prices. However, entire industries would be crippled, and there would be numerous other problems. My solution is just that: a solution. There are many best-of-breed solutions that I simply don't have the resources or knowledge to create.

Your job as CEO is to provide your company with the best-of-breed solutions, not just "a" solution. When a CEO treats their own solutions as if they are best-of-breed solutions, this is Peacock Management. The CEO struts around like a proud peacock, feathers all up in the air, but although the show might be splendid, not much is actually accomplished.

REAL-LIFE EXAMPLE

Jack was a powerful leader, a decisive CEO who prided himself on his "ready, fire, aim" philosophy. Some of Jack's key people called his style "fire, ready, aim" instead. After five years of excellent growth and profitability, Jack found his business contracting when a competitor began taking away his key accounts. Upon examination, Jack discovered that the competitor had a lower cost structure through better logistics. Jack was surprised to discover this as he had led his company's logistics upgrade two years before. After much pain and lost profit, Jack realized that his logistics upgrade was the best that HE knew, not the best the universe of business people knew. His competitor had hired a high-caliber logistics person to implement their program, and this expert created a system that gave his competitor an advantage. Jack learned that best-of-breed practices rarely come from one's own organization.

SOLUTION

Create outlets to gain access to industry and general business best practices. One of my clients has a great saying: "I want to assume everything I am doing is WRONG," which is the exact opposite of how most confident CEOs think. Most CEOs work from the presumption that their ideas are right and/or best-of-breed, which on occasion causes them to forge ahead with false confidence.

Let's face it. We all have a bias that most ideas we generate are brilliant. Confidence is great, but let us temper it with a fervent pursuit of industry/business best practices.

Fatal Error #8:
Teetering on Greatness

Running a business can be a challenging and frustrating task. This task can be made significantly easier by following the adage "surround yourself with good people." However, some CEOs take this too far. Good people make your life easy as CEO, but the problem is that good people command good pay. Your organization may be too top-heavy and have a cost structure that creates a cost disadvantage. Your business may actually be teetering under the cost burden of your quality people.

Virtually every industry has significant cost pressure. One way to meet this cost pressure is to lower your wage structure. The best way to lower your wage structure is to leverage your good people. If you have too many good people, you are under-leveraged by definition. An under-leveraged organization looks like this:

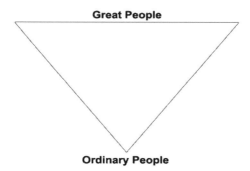

Great People

Ordinary People

That is, lots of great people for every "ordinary person." However, your customer wants your organization to look like this:

That is, a few great people leveraging the "ordinary people." The customer wants YOU to figure out how to significantly leverage your talent pool by having the lowest paid and lowest skilled employees possible doing the task while maintaining the same level of quality. This, by definition, keeps costs down.

REAL-LIFE EXAMPLE

Izzy's IT consulting company had grown to 20 people in only seven years. Izzy had a knack for picking top talent and had seven key employees who were all capable of running their own firm. Obviously, Izzy had to pay these seven employees quite well. For the jobs the seven performed, they were overpaid 20% above market rates. However, the seven were exceptional with customers, did outstanding work, and were trouble-free employees.

As Izzy's company continued to grow, pricing pressure became an issue. Izzy realized the seven key employees made his life "easy" but were a cost burden. Izzy came to the conclusion that he must lower his cost structure to continue to grow the business, that the seven had to be cut or leverage added to their work. This leverage could be accomplished by adding subordinates to the key seven or increasing the "value" of the work produced by these seven employees.

Izzy decided to cease hiring top-level people and work to develop subordinates for his key seven people. Over the next year, Izzy's firm grew to 25 people. The five additional employees were bottom level people, thereby lowering the overall cost structure.

SOLUTION

Your job as CEO is NOT to make your life easy. Your job is to service your customer. It is a safe bet that your customers are pounding you for lower and lower pricing, and consequently, like it or not, you MUST better leverage your quality people. Training is key to this process. Most organizations provide poor training to their employees and compensate by hiring "great people" who don't need to be trained. This is nothing more than path-of-least-resistance thinking. It is easier today to hire great people, but you pay for it with the unending pressure of an uncompetitive cost structure.

I know, adding more lower-skilled "knuckleheads" to your payroll curdles your blood. For what it is worth, I am sure there is some manager at NASA saying, "Why are all these rocket scientists such knuckleheads?" It is just human nature. You have two choices when it comes to leveraging your talent base. First, you can say, "Forget you, Jim. I want my life to be easy and great employees make my life easy." Okay, that is a fair and valid answer, but you are hereby forbidden from complaining about profits, margins, or prima donna employees. You picked the path.

Second, you can pick the leverage path. The leveraged path has challenges making lower-skilled employees productive and profitable. There is no right answer here. It is your business, which means it is your choice. Conventional wisdom says you should pick the second option though. For what it is worth, I believe leveraging a company and still delivering excellent service/value is one of the most difficult tasks an owner faces. The owners who are successful create a business with tremendous salability and value.

NOTES:

_____

_____

_____

_____

_____

_____

_____

_____

_____

_____

Fatal Error #9: Smalketing

How many salespeople have you employed like this? Please don't say "all of them." If that is the case, you might need to take ownership of this issue rather than your salespeople being accountable for the situation.

Many entrepreneurs confuse sales and marketing. For simplicity's sake, marketing brings the prospect to you with a desire to buy, which is sometimes referred to as "pull." Sales require that prospective business be actively sought out, which is sometimes referred to as "push." Most products need to be sold because the buyers do not come to you. Too many salespeople sit around waiting for the phone to ring. Selling converts prospects into customers while marketing brings in new prospects. Most businesses need both activities.

The real problem occurs when sales go south, and the CEO then says, "We need more marketing." Many times, more selling is what is needed. First, however, you need to truly understand whether you move product by marketing or selling. Ask yourself, "If the best salesperson in the world walked through the door tomorrow, could she get more business?" The answer is almost always "yes" because there are lots of prospects that have not been "worked" and deals that could have been closed.

Here is how you can tell whether marketing or sales is more important (pick one): A) your sales force is nothing but superstars but you cannot market AT ALL; or B) you have salespeople like the cartoon but your marketing is stellar. Which method generates more sales? If it is A, then your product needs to be sold. If it is B, then marketing is more important. For instance, Crest toothpaste is not "sold" in stores but marketed on television.

For many small companies, sales is what is needed. More marketing only exacerbates the problem. It is like the old adage: "a great ad campaign will make a bad product fail faster."[4] Why bring in more prospects who do not buy?

REAL-LIFE EXAMPLE

Clay asked me to look at the sales function of his software company because he wanted to make sure he was not leaving sales on the table. Clay's sales "seemed" to be growing more than adequately. When I observed his five salespeople, I found they spent most of their time in the office and virtually no time cold calling. They simply worked the leads that came to them. When I asked Clay if the customers came to him or they needed to chase the business, he said, "The business definitely needs to be chased." By realigning the sales force by converting one salesperson to a telemarketer, Clay reduced costs but also dramatically increased the number of leads fed to his salespeople.

---

4   Bernbach, William & Higins, Denis. *The Art of Writing Advertising* (Advertising Publications, 1965), p.23

SOLUTION

You may need more marketing, but before you market, closely examine your existing prospects and, if necessary, rework them. Change account reps for problem accounts or bring in a new salesperson. Always "shake things up" on the sales front before investing in marketing.

If your organization is strong in sales, skip ahead. For those of you whose businesses are strong in something other than sales, here is an observation: Employees who don't "get" sales have two Achilles heels. First, they "presuppose the hard part." Every product or service has some facet of sales or marketing that is especially important or difficult. For instance, everyone knows the retail axiom "location, location, location." That is the hard part and it should not be underestimated or undervalued. For most businesses, generating a quality prospect is the "hard part." Most businesses I have been around do well once they get their hands on the quality prospect. However, show me a company that is struggling with sales and I'll bet they presuppose the quality prospect. They say things like, "People should be buying from us, our customer service is great." Who cares? No one BUYS because of great service. They STAY because of great service. Great service gets you no customers. Sorry to be blunt, but you are probably putting WAY (10 times) too little effort into new quality prospect acquisition.

The Achilles heel on the other foot is that employees who don't get sales GROSSLY underestimate the value of a prospect. Let's play a game. I have the ability to instantly deliver an A-list customer to you. This new customer is ideal — they will stay with your firm as long as you retain one of your average customers and their margins will be equal to your typical margin. They will spend 20% less in dollars than your best customer, but they WILL buy for sure. Now, the only way to get this customer is to write me a check. You cannot get the customer ANY other way. Roll with me here. How much will you pay? $1,000? $5,000? $100,000? Write it down. CEOs who are strong in areas other than sales GROSSLY undervalue the customer.

For example, a $500,000 annual customer stays for two years on average and provides 30% gross margin. This will add as much as $300,000 to your profit. Paying $5,000 for $300,000 in profit is way too little. I have a friend who is a senior partner at a large accounting firm. He counsels his clients that, in many businesses, it takes one-third the lifetime gross profit to acquire a new client. Based on our scenario and his formula, you should be willing to pay $100,000 cold, hard cash for the client. Let's take that one step further: what is a quality prospect worth? If you close only 10% of the prospects (I am NOT talking qualified prospects here — you have to have a raw prospect before you can have a qualified one), this raw prospect is worth spending $10,000 to acquire.

I use this illustration for a reason. Strong sales types get this. Weak sales types don't get it. Ask yourself, were you willing to spend the $10,000 to generate a prospect that MIGHT buy? My guess is no. Is this the reason you are not selling enough?

Sales is not the "black art" you think it is. Ask someone who is strong in sales and they will tell you it is simple. Sales and sales management IS pretty simple. It only seems complicated because your sales process is probably weak and you probably stink at picking salespeople. Good salespeople know what a good salesperson looks, smells, and acts like. There is an old adage: "What is every salesperson best at selling? Themselves." CEOs who are not "sales types" always get burned by this. If you can't figure out how to sniff out the snow-jobbers, hire a headhunter or HR person to do it for you!

NOTES:

_____

_____

_____

_____

_____

_____

_____

Fatal Error #10: "We Suck" Selling

When I survey businesses, margin pressure is always #1 on the complaint list. It seems that everyone is susceptible to lowering their price to gain or keep market share. Don't do it! When you lower your price you are saying, "Yeah, we have so little to offer the customer that we have no other option but to lower the price."

REAL-LIFE EXAMPLE

Tamara was in the alarm business. Her "most productive" salesperson, Bill, accounted for 50% of total sales. For years, Tamara left Bill alone because he was generating new business. However, upon closer inspection, Bill was drastically under-pricing his bids. Some bids were 30% lower than the competition. To make matters worse, Bill was crossing out key elements of the alarm monitoring contract that could destroy the profitability of a specific job if negative events occurred. Upon the advice of her CEO group, Tamara told Bill that cross-outs would no longer be accepted. Bill ignored her and continued as he had previously, but he was still bringing in new business so Tamara ignored it. After six months, Tamara got serious and reasserted her position. Bill continued to bring in contracts with items crossed out. Her CEO group suggested Tamara buy a lighter and have another conversion with Bill. With lighter in hand, Tamara told Bill that the next contract with cross-outs would be burned on the spot. Bill got the message. However, Bill's deals were still too cheap, and Tamara began to pressure him to bring better deals. Eventually, Bill quit. He was incapable of selling without "giving it away." Tamara hired a solid replacement for Bill. Deal volume was lower, but the dramatic increase in margin more than made up for it.

SOLUTION

Beware! The solution is not as simple as holding your ground on pricing. If you are feeling price pressure, you must increase your VALUE to avoid lowering your price. Remember, "value" is defined by the customers. Think of pricing like a teeter-totter. If you are feeling like you need to lower your price, it is a sign that something is wrong with your value equation. Instead of "adding weight" to the price side of the equation, add features or value, which can allow you to hold your price.

Sales prices are determined by a variety of factors: market maturity, market competitiveness, age and strength of competitors, need to acquire new business, availability of alternatives and branding. You may have more leverage on your customers than you think. Your product/service may be differentiated from other products so that you can command a premium for it. In his book *Double Digit Growth,*[5] Michael Treacy states that you must be able to steal business from your competitors with your value proposition. If you cannot, you need to re-think your value proposition and your differentiation.

Entrepreneurs tell me all the time what their customers SHOULD value. Stop drinking your own Kool-Aid! That is, if your customers aren't buying your PR, stop buying it yourself. Here is a simple rule: pay attention to the customers' WALLET, not their mouth. Customers "vote" with their wallet. If they aren't "voting," nothing else matters. Tinker with your value equation until they vote with their wallet.

BONUS

Visit *www.mysalesmap.com* for ideas.

---

5   Treacy, Michael. *Double Digit Growth: How Great Companies Achieve It, No Matter What.* (New York: Penguin Group, 2003), p. 128.

Fatal Error #11:
Herding Cats

The customer is always right? HOGWASH! It depends on how you define "right." I define "right" as a modifier for "customer" this way: provides the vendor with reasonable profit, is not overly demanding, does not create unnecessary emergencies, treats the vendor's people well, etc. If you allow the customer to always be "right," you allow the customer to completely dictate the terms of the relationship and create one-off transactions. When you allow the customer to consistently create one-off transactions, you are herding cats, a famously inefficient activity. When you herd cats in the business sense, you create a high-cost, low-efficiency model that is not good for you or for the customer. The cat herding model creates an incentive for the customer to switch to a vendor that better manages the process and keeps costs down. Therefore, by trying too hard to give any given customer everything they THINK they want, you actually drive the customer away.

Just because the customer gives you money does not give them carte blanch to dictate every other business term. It is not against the rules for you to help the customer to help you. Isn't that the definition of a win-win scenario? What would happen if you set upfront expectations with your customer? By educating your customer how to be a better customer for you, you enhance the vendor-customer relationship. Educated correctly, your customer will become a profitable partner in your business.

REAL-LIFE EXAMPLE

Donnie sold specialized computer hardware to eye doctors and his installations were across the country, so customer support was tricky from Chicago. It seemed that every time there was a minor issue, Donnie's company became the scapegoat. Most of the problems were nothing more than user error, but users were bad-mouthing Donnie's

company and hurting referral opportunities. Worse yet, once the system was installed, the doctors relied on their error-prone staff to use the equipment. The staff was poisoning Donnie's company's reputation with eye doctors. As a result, Donnie began a client education program. Clients were told that there would be rough patches at first, and users were better trained and given a technical hotline to head off issues. Doctors were educated that user errors were common immediately following installation. The result was a 135% improvement in client satisfaction and a rebound in referrals.

SOLUTION

Think hard about what a perfect customer does for you aside from the money they give you. A partial list includes:

- Easy to do business with
- Provides a reasonable margin
- Provides sales during a slow time
- Provides a base of business
- Pays promptly
- Not overly demanding of customer support and few issues
- Buys high-margin items

- Readily self-serve (for example, track their own package on the FedEx website, fill their own drink at McDonalds, readily delivers carts from the lot as Wal-Mart asks to keep payroll down)

The above items are rarely negotiated with the customer. That is, the terms remain unspoken, and therefore undemanded, which favors the buyer. For instance, who has ever sat down at the negotiating table and said, "Mr. Customer, how much customer support time are you going to need, because if you need too much, I have to raise your price." It does not work this way, we charge all customers the same, no matter whether they tax our customer service department or pay poorly. I like to call these "non-cash terms." If you ignore the non-cash terms, the customer gets the better end of the bargain. If you set terms up front and educate your customer about how to have a better win-win scenario, you **WILL** become more profitable.

Like it or not, in every transaction, one party is the puppet and the other is the puppeteer, and which party plays which role boils down to who has the leverage. Typically, the person waving the money around has the leverage, but not always. For instance, doctors are very good at dictating that customers play by their rules, and thereby, they are good at playing the puppeteer. Many doctors ask you to:

- Show up on time or pay a fee
- Pay if you miss the appointment
- Wait for them in their "queue" so they can operate at maximum efficiency while you waste your time
- Work with their assistants vs. the doctor (e.g., to take your blood pressure, etc.)
- Come to their office vs. them coming to you even though you are ill
- Prove that you have the financial means to pay before you are even seen by the doctor

These measures improve the profitability of the doctor's practice while not ticking you off enough to go to another provider.

Now look at your business from the customer's perspective and see which of your items are reasonable to ask of them. If you want maximum profitability, you MUST be the puppeteer. If you are not currently the puppeteer, figure out what is wrong with your value equation and fix it. Asking your customers to help you increase profits or reduce costs is NOT unreasonable. Profits indirectly benefit the customer by creating margin for you without raising prices.

Twenty-five percent of CEOs have not educated their customers because they have not thought to do it. Seventy-five percent of CEOs have not educated their customers because they are CHICKEN, simply afraid that their customers may buy somewhere else if they try to ask for more. Be brutally honest with yourself: Are you simply afraid, or are you afraid for a reason? Is the total value proposition you provide to the customer so weak that your success teeters on the possibility of losing their business?

One of the most important business dynamics in the next five years will be "controlling the customer." Stated more stridently: the businesses that will be the MOST successful will learn to control their customers. You gain control of the customer by providing a superior basket of value that the competition cannot duplicate.

Once you have gained control of the customer, you have the ability to dictate terms and play the puppeteer. Don't take this the wrong way. Dictating terms does not have to be a negative. Dictating terms is what the doctor was doing in the example above. It allows the doctor to be more profitable with a small amount of discomfort to his or her patients.

The best companies have grabbed control of the customer and used this control to dictate terms. For instance, there is a Wal-Mart across the street from my daughter's dance studio. If I am killing time, I sometimes make the mistake of buying something at this particular Wal-Mart. Virtually every time I have bought something at this store I have tolerated the following lousy conditions: not enough carts, a dirty store, fifteen or more people in every checkout line, no customer service, etc. Yet I keep going back. Why? Wal-Mart has the location I need and I know I won't overpay. This "basket of values" allows them to dictate all the above business terms to me: "Jim, you are going to wait in a long line and waste a significant amount of your time because we don't want to pay more cashiers." "Jim, you might not get a cart because we don't pay enough staff to fetch them for you." "Jim, if you want your low, everyday prices, here are the non-cash terms."

Need more? How about your cell phone company? They woo you, indeed entice the daylights out of you, to get you "in." Once you are a customer, you only talk to people whose first language is not English and wait forever for customer service. These non-cash terms help their profitability. Have you switched providers because of it? Nope. You might switch for price or service area, but cell phone companies KNOW this. They KNOW you will tolerate crappy customer service in exchange for coverage area and price.

Here is what you can do: figure out where your prospects vote with their wallet. Remember, complaints come out of the mouth; money comes out of the wallet. Strengthen the value you offer the customer. Then figure out how the customer can save you money with a small amount of pain on their part, and then ask your client to give you these non-cash terms. Better yet, grab control of the customer with compelling value and DEMAND they give them to you.

BONUS

Visit *51errors.com/packet.html* for sample Customer Education Packets.

Fatal Error #12:
It Ain't Worth What You Think

You are going to hate me for this one: Fifty percent of small businesses have little or no value outside of real estate. There are two reasons for this: 1) The business cannot effectively and/or profitably operate without the owner; 2) The owner's take from the business is not much better than a job.

Who would pay you $500,000 for a $75,000 a year job? The buyer of your business could get a $75,000 job for $0. The buyer would not have to work 60 hours per week either. The only way to make your business worth the money it should be worth is to get it into a position where it makes significant money **WITHOUT** your direct daily input.

Let's have some fun here. Let's say I represent a venture firm with $50 million to invest. Today I am in the investing mood and want to buy your business. How much do I pay you? Don't read ahead. Think of your answer. Write it down. I write you the check. You celebrate like there is no tomorrow. Everything is great. Three days from now, I come to you and say,

> *"Hey, we were excited about taking the business to another level, and we had a plan and a team in place to do it, but our team fell apart and we won't be able to take over your business. Now, I certainly don't expect you to give me my money back. However, I would like it if you would buy it back for a fair price.*

What is that price? What is the first number that comes out of your head? Was it the same number you sold it for? I already know the answer: it wasn't. You already know where I am going. It's worth the lower number.

THE 51 FATAL BUSINESS ERRORS — AND HOW TO AVOID THEM

I do this exercise live at workshops and have had some entertaining conversations. I did the exercise with a guy in Kentucky. His sale price was $18 million. His buyback price was $2 million. In another situation, the gentleman told me it would take $12 million to buy his business. When I asked how much he would buy it back for, he said, "Hey, a deal is a deal." He would not even buy the turkey back.

REAL-LIFE EXAMPLE

Sandy and her husband had run a woodworking tool distributorship for nearly twenty years. Sandy decided it was time to retire. When I asked, "How much do you think the business is worth?" She answered, "One million dollars." I challenged her: she could not afford to pay herself more than $60,000 per year, the business was breaking even, Home Depot and franchises were eroding her customer base, and key manufacturing customers were moving their operations to China. When she asked what she could get for the business, she did not like my answer. I felt no one would buy a $60,000 job for any price and that the best course of action was to systematically liquidate the $350,000 worth of inventory she owned free and clear. On her short timetable, this was Sandy's best option.

SOLUTION

Alright, this is a "duh," but it is true. Your business is only worth what someone will pay for it. **The best tactic for selling your business is to have it run well and profitably without your direct involvement.** I am guessing you already knew this but have not done much about it. Therefore, further enlightenment is probably not needed, so read the Mule-kick on the next page.

Sometimes, people are afraid to make this bet. Come on, be brave enough to hold yourself accountable for the great results you can and WILL deliver.

I realize that removing yourself from the day-to-day operations is difficult. I realize that things "don't go right" when you are not involved. However, you are selling yourself short by doing day-to-day TASKS that don't move your business forward but only keep it from moving backward. Think of how lousy you will feel five years from now if your major business accomplishment is "not going backward." You can do better than that, but you have to do what I call "making a bet on yourself." Most of the time, getting yourself out of these tasks involves spending money, perhaps buying automation or hiring help. Either way, you have to reach in your wallet and say, "I can add more value to the business by spending this money to get my time back."

BONUS

Visit *51errors.com/valuation.html* for a value calculator to estimate the true value of your business.

NOTES:

_____

_____

_____

_____

Fatal Error #13:
Saving Your Way to Success

If you analyze your expenses for the past three years, you will probably find a maximum of 10% potential savings in your expenses. This is not bad money, but it is not enough to make you rich. The real money is in the top line. Attempting to save your way to success stems from laziness. Trimming expenses is step one in a two-step process. Increasing the top line is the second step. Cutting expenses will only solve part of the problem.

Additionally, the money-conscious CEO treats the purchase of anything outside the ordinary course of business as a waste of money. Most of these "wastes of money" involve long-term improvement of the business or sharpening the saw (for instance, a large investment in new software or a major re-branding). The most successful CEOs invest (not spend) heavily in the future of their business.

REAL-LIFE EXAMPLE

Tom quit his accounting practice to buy one of his client's businesses. Immediately, Tom was able to improve the profitability dramatically by cutting expenses. However, Tom's focus on expenses and lack of concentration on sales eventually caught up with him. Sales trickled downward to the point the business could not remain profitable. Tom tried to cut expenses again, but only small gains were made. The situation could not be rectified without increasing sales.

SOLUTION

Spend lavishly on STRATEGIC investments. Invest in sales and marketing. Invest in ideas: both your internal company ideas and those of experts. Monitor and keep tabs on your expenses, but profitable top-line growth will always trump expense cutting.

A CEO who keeps trying to cut costs to increase profits is engaged in what I call "over-juicing the lemon." You over-juice the lemon when you hit the point of diminishing returns yet keep going. Aside from cutting costs, CEOs over-juice the lemon by trying to get too much business from a customer or milking a dying product.

NOTES:

_____

_____

_____

_____

_____

_____

_____

_____

Fatal Error #14:
Paying Yourself Below Market Value

I f this does not apply to you, good. Skip ahead. When times get bad, some executives stop paying themselves. This can eventually create a big problem, an artificial subsidy that you are granting the business. This is effectively an off-balance-sheet loan from you to the company. Typically, this loan is never repaid and the money just disappears. The only problem is that this is YOUR money. Moreover, usually the executive continues to underpay himself long after the crisis has ended, which is just a smaller artificial subsidy.

REAL-LIFE EXAMPLE

Gil's business was off to a good start. He had great customers and solid growth. Even three years after starting the business, Gil simply did not feel justified curbing the growth by taking a salary. The profits on paper continued. Growth continued. Gil continued not taking a salary. Eventually, lack of personal income cramped Gil's style enough to look for a change. I challenged Gil to take a small $30,000 salary and see what happened. To Gil's surprise, the growth of the business was not stymied. Gil continued over time to raise his salary to $100,000 without damaging the growth of the business. Gil now realizes that a growing business **NEVER** has enough cash. Paying himself last only fed the beast a bit more but did not satisfy the cash appetite of a growing business.

SOLUTION

What would you have to pay someone to do your job? That is what you should pay yourself no matter what the times. To underpay yourself creates an artificial reality. Yes, underpaying yourself makes it easier to dig out of the hole, but such a strategy may also extend the time it takes to dig out. Why? You have tricked yourself into thinking the hole is smaller than it actually is. Your salary represents some of that hole. Count your salary as part of what you will need to dig out of the hole.

If you want to stop paying yourself, set an end date to this arrangement before you cut off the paychecks. If you are not able to resume paying yourself on that date, you have some tough questions to answer. Can the business make it without your artificial subsidy? What could you make working for someone else? **Sometimes, ceasing to pay yourself only camouflages the real issues.**

NOTES:

_____

_____

_____

_____

_____

_____

_____

CHAPTER 3

Is It Time to Fire Your C.E.O.?

(Yes, I'm Talking About You)

One of the reasons we entrepreneurs love our job is the control. We love being the captain of our own ship. However, effectively captaining a ship or running a business requires hundreds, if not thousands, of individual skills. Guess what! You can't excel at all of them! Therefore, if you want your business to improve, you have to improve your captaining ability.

When it comes down to it, EVERYTHING is your fault. Even if your people let you down, who hired them? Who trained them? Who trusted them? You get my point. If you want to dramatically improve the effectiveness of your business, you have to DRAMATICALLY improve the effectiveness of you.

In Lewis Carroll's *Alice in Wonderland,* the Mad Hatter appeared to Alice to be a very important person. However, the Hatter ran around saying, "I'm late, I'm late, for a VERY important date." The Mad Hatter was so busy running around that he literally could not even remember what he was late for.

Sometimes we run our businesses like the Mad Hatter. We run around stomping out the fires of the day and forget to engage in the meaningful activities that will drive long-term value. When we settle for fighting the fire-of-the-day, we hamper the long-term growth of our business. We are working *in* our business, not *on* our business. That is, we have a job, not a business. Robert Kiyosaki, in his book, *Rich Dad, Poor Dad,* lays out this premise: "A business pays an investment return WITHOUT your direct involvement."

The following errors provide some insight into how you can begin to improve your performance and effectiveness as CEO of your company.

NOTES:

_____

_____

_____

_____

_____

_____

_____

_____

Fatal Error #15:
Managing Subjectively

As a consultant, I frequently joke with my clients, "I am a rocket scientist on this side of the desk, but I am a moron on that side." A business is much easier to run if it is not personal (that is, subjective). Before you YABUT me (see Error # 42), it is IMPOSSIBLE to run YOUR OWN business objectively. Your business will always be subjective to you, but you must learn to run it as objectively as possible. Ask yourself, "If I hired the best person in the world to run this business, what would they do?"

Andy Grove and Gordon Moore asked themselves this very question in the late 1970s. Intel was a successful memory chip company, but growth had slowed and prices were cutthroat. Moore and Grove thought that if the best CEO in the world were running Intel, he or she would exit the memory chip business, and that is exactly what they did.[6] They refocused the company on higher margin items like CPUs and the rest is history. As an aside, the memory chip business WAS their business, and Moore and Grove effectively quit their existing business and started anew.

I am not suggesting that you trash your core business. However, it is a safe bet that the best CEO in the world would not run the business in the exact same manner you do.

REAL-LIFE EXAMPLE

Lesley was a key employee for John and had been an important part of the business's success to this point. However, lately, Lesley's personal issues began to affect her work, and rather than improving with time, the situation got worse. John would periodically have a talk with Lesley, but these talks had no long-lasting effect. John's friends

---

6   Miller, Stacy Lynne. *Revival of the Fittest* (PublishAmerica, July 3, 2006), p.110

and family suggested that Lesley be fired. John had a very difficult time doing this because of Lesley's history with the company. In particular, John remembered his hospital stay when Lesley kept the business going.

To an objective party, it was clear that Lesley needed to be fired. However, John was incapable of being objective. Lesley's performance continued to erode over time. Finally, Lesley was insubordinate to a client causing the client to switch vendors. John called this the "last straw" and fired Lesley. Eventually, John got a coach to use as a sounding board. Over time, John was able to learn how to manage more objectively.

SOLUTION

The best way to learn to be more objective is to "get a fresh pair of eyeballs" such as a consultant, a board of directors, or hiring someone outside your company or industry. Of course, you have to listen to the outsiders you hire or you will only get more of the same. Learning to become more objective happens one situation at a time. Each time you use your sounding board AND listen to them, you become more objective.

Never in the history of business has a CEO said, "Gosh, I fired them too soon."

BONUS

Visit *51errors.com/management.html* for a self-assessment exercise. This exercise will help you diagnose how you can manage more objectively.

Fatal Error #16:
Wearing the Dog Collar

Every business owner dreams of the day a $50,000,000 check slides across the table to them. I've seen checks with a lot of zeros slide to my clients; it is great! By the same token, I have seen many talented entrepreneurial CEOs bogged down in a moderately profitable business. They work too hard for their money and are not overly satisfied with the work. A CEO who is underutilized and working below their true value and skill level is, as I am inclined to describe them, "wearing the dog collar."

There are several layers to this concept, so I will start at the core. Every activity you personally perform in your business has a dollar value. If you do the books, this value may be the cost savings to the organization of hiring an accountant. If you are managing people, the value may be the increased productivity of your subordinates. If you are closing a sale, it may be the increased revenue to the company. Here is a partial list of activities you can perform to add value to your company:

- Job functions (saves money by eliminating payroll to others)
- Planning/strategy (creates opportunities for the organization)
- Marketing/sales (creates revenue)
- Management (improves productivity)
- Standard bearer (the most important role of a CEO. The standard bearer enforces the culture and quality standards for all aspects of the organization. This is not only the quality of the product/service but the quality of every activity performed within the organization. The CEO may communicate the standards personally or through managers.)
- Systems creation and implementation (systems automate your business and eliminate the need for your personal input and oversight)

- Un-done activities (what is the opportunity cost of the activities you are NOT doing in lieu of the ones you are?)

This task/activity value will become the y-axis, or vertical axis, of our grid. The x-axis, or horizontal axis, of the grid is the time and frequency of these activities. For instance, if you work on the books one hour per month, that saves $75 per month. If you work on the books ten hours per month, you save $750 per month. Of course, there is an opportunity cost associated with doing the books, which will be shown in the grid below.

The chart below is called The Delegation Grid. Of course, turning yourself into a high-value CEO is more complex than just delegation. However, the crux of delegation is "I am not going to do this because I am worth more than this task." That is what this grid is about, your value to the organization. In order for you to drive your business to the next level, you must focus on high-impact, high-value tasks. The simplest way to rid yourself of low-impact, low-value tasks is to delegate.

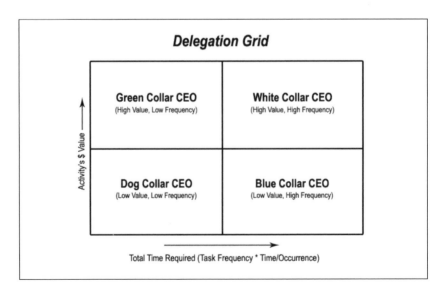

Every CEO wears four "collars" at some point during the year, if not monthly or even daily:

- The Blue Collar
  - These activities are frequently-occurring low-value-added activities.
  - Examples:
    - ~ Driving a route truck regularly
    - ~ Filling what should be a staff position
    - ~ Spending a day at the customer service desk because someone called in sick
    - ~ Serving as the primary point of contact for a low-value customer
    - ~ Running errands, such as picking up office supplies, delivering customer orders, or picking up parts/supplies
    - ~ Low-impact or repetitious sales activities
- The White Collar
  - These activities are frequently-occurring high-value activities. Do not confuse the traditional blue collar/white collar distinctions. For this model, the only relevancy is the value of the work to the organization. For instance, a secretarial job is white collar at a construction company, but the skilled laborers have a higher dollar value to the organization. In this example, it could be that the secretarial job is blue collar and the construction job is white collar depending on the values associated.
  - Examples:
    - ~ Many management activities. Most CEOs start off with all the management activities, and as the business grows, the lower-value activities get delegated to other managers
    - ~ Serving as the primary point of contact for a high-value customer
    - ~ Most high-impact sales activities

- ~ High-impact financial activities such as banking relationships
- ~ High-impact operational activities
- The Green Collar
  - These activities are low-frequency but very high-value activities.
  - Most of these activities fall under Leadership.
  - Examples:
    - ~ Planning/Strategy
    - ~ Management of key staff
    - ~ Standard bearer
    - ~ Dreamer/Creator
    - ~ Futurist. The futurist understands the upcoming political, industrial, economic, and technological landscape. He or she then translates this understanding and prognostication into a direction for the company.
    - ~ Motivator/Inspirer
- The Dog Collar
  - These activities are the ones that trap you. They are low-value and low-frequency.
  - Most delegation theories fail to take the dog collar activities into account. Typical delegation theory can be summarized something like this: "If you can pay someone else to do it for you, you should do so." Overall, this is good advice, but any CEO who has been in business a week knows this is IMPOSSIBLE. The fallacy of standard delegation theory is that the task frequency is not taken into account. For example, Bill spends ½ hour per month bookkeeping. On the surface, this is $40 per hour work and is far below his expertise/value. Yet, he still does this work. Why? Because it is more complicated than simply offloading $40 per hour work. These are Bill's finances, so there is a cost to opening

his books to an outsider. There is a handoff cost in simply explaining the work to someone else. Bill figures he would only save a few minutes passing off the work, so he chooses to do it himself. He chooses to wear the dog collar in this instance. WE ALL DO. The trick is to minimize our time wearing said collar, not to eliminate it altogether. As the frequency increases, this may allow Bill to delegate the task.

— Examples:

  ~ If you regularly fill in driving a route truck, this is Blue Collar. If you fill in for an emergency, this is Dog Collar
  ~ Stuck fulfilling the duties of a position you can't fill
  ~ Playing the backup role for some positions; stop-gap

Value is a tricky computation for the grid. First, you subjectively set the value. There is no "right" answer. Second, opportunity cost needs to enter the equation. For instance, if you are a superstar sales-type, you could spend all day selling and generate excellent value for the organization. However, what do you sacrifice? What you are sacrificing could be worth more to the organization than the selling activity generates. Third, the value scale is individual. That is, you have your scale and I have mine. To you, an activity might need to generate $5,000 per hour to be Green Collar, but for me it might only be $3,000 per hour.

The next step is to draw the delegation line. The delegation line will help you decide which activates should be done by you and which should be done by others. The white area above the line represents activities that you SHOULD do. The gray area below the line represents activities you should NOT do. We all have activities we are doing that are "below the line." Don't fret. The first step is to become aware of it, but the second step is to recognize that every activity you are doing below the line is HOLDING YOU BACK! Every activity you do below the line sells yourself, and thereby your business, short. Here is a graphical representation of a delegation line.

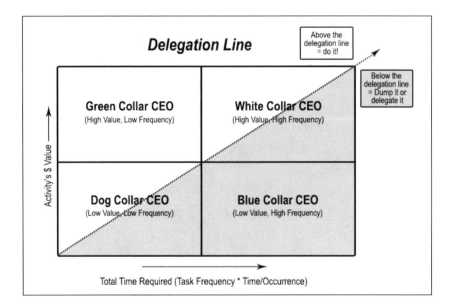

The next step in the process is to figure out the slope of your line. Fill in the blanks on the Delegation Prep form below. An example chart is below as well.

On the top of the vertical axis of the blank Delegation Grid (below) write the highest dollar amount from question #4. This represents the top of your scale. Now, from question #4, plot the values of your activities along the value axis (vertical axis) and the time axis (horizontal axis). For the time axis, guess how much time a month (or a year) you spend doing the task. This is arbitrary, but I have set the top of the time scale at 50% of your time. Most CEOs do not spend 50% of their time on any one task. Feel free to adjust this scale to better fit your situation. Repeat for question #5 but skip #6. Question #6 is included to show you how much "upside" you have. Mark all 10 points on the chart. Draw the line in the middle. That is, draw the line so that five points are above the line and five points are below the line. In the example below, I put four above and six below so it would better represent the true delegation line. Page 76 shows the above example charted.

Sample Delegation Prep

                                        % of Time

1. Write down how much you make (salary + profits) in a year $200,000

2. Divide by 2000 (the approximate number of hours in a year)

3. This is your approximate current value per hour $100

4. Write down the 5 most important activities you do for the company & their value per hour

Handle largest customer as sales rep	$200	30%
Annual planning & strategy	$500	5%
Host corporate retreat	$300	5%
Face-person for the company	$250	15%
Fill the role of CIO	$75	10%

5. Write down the 5 least important activities you do for the company & their value per hour

Deal with IT vendors	$ 50	5%
Fill in for missing staff	$45	10%
Take deposits to bank	$15	2%
Hire entry level staff	$40	5%
Accounting work	$40	5%

6. Write down the 3 highest impact activities you COULD do for the company or could do more of but are not currently doing & their value per hour

Spend more time with large customers	$400
Spearhead key product initiative	$1,000
Retool marketing program	$300

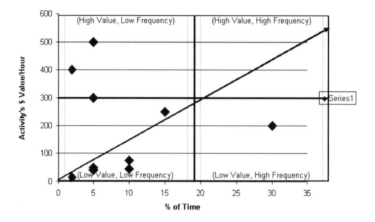

Here is a blank grid for you to chart your own delegation line.

Delegation Grid

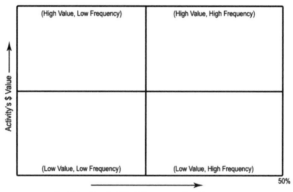

Total Time Required (Task Frequency * Time/Occurrence)

The Green Collar CEO

A Green Collar CEO is a highly effective and highly profitable business leader who spends very little of her time on low-impact items. Green Collar CEOs are highly entrepreneurial multi-taskers. They are adept at managing multiple priorities while maintaining maximum efficiency.

Most importantly, a Green Collar CEO understands that she directly and indirectly drives every dollar of profit for the organization. With this great responsibility, the Green Collar CEO spends her time doing the activities that only she can truly do. Neither she, nor her organization can afford her to spend time on the day-to-day work of the business.

Lastly, Green Collar CEOs get paid exceptionally well. When an entrepreneur learns the method of becoming a Green Collar CEO, their value to their organization grows exponentially and their pay rises with it.

Just the opposite is true for the Blue Collar CEO. The Blue Collar CEO spends a large amount of time on low-value tasks. Since the tasks don't add much value to the organization, the only way to delegate them is to find help that is sufficiently cheap enough, which creates a catch-22 in situations where qualified cheap help is difficult to find, effectively trapping the CEO in those tasks. Been there, done that, right?

As you can see from the graph below, the trajectory of your delegation line determines what type of CEO you are currently. There is a direct correlation between your delegation line and your income/success. Think what Donald Trump's Delegation Line must look like. It would almost be 90° straight up. Your duty as CEO is to continually move your line closer to 90°.

So, what moves the line counterclockwise? The bad news is that the delegation line is about you. It is personal. Therefore, the slope of your delegation line has much more to do with you than your company, but of course your company is a reflection of you and so the two are not easily separated as regards the outcome of your delegation practices. The bottom line is that moving the line depends on your actions. The factors that move the line are as follows:

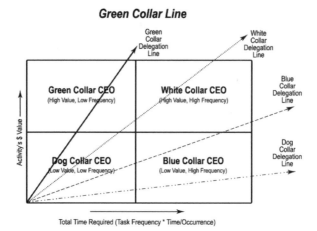

Green Collar Line

Total Time Required (Task Frequency * Time/Occurrence)

- Maturity of the company. Mature companies tend to have more:
  - Availability of human capital.
  - Availability of financial capital.
  - Viable training systems within the company.
- Risk tolerance
  - The higher your risk tolerance, the steeper your delegation line.
  - Long-term or short-term payoff. The time to reward affects how much risk you can take.
  - Likelihood of the payoff. Risk takers tend to see payoffs that are higher than do risk avoiders.
- Perfectionism
  - Your need to have everything "just right" will push your delegation line the wrong way.
- Micromanagement
  - Needing to have your finger in everything will also push your delegation line the wrong way.
- CEO's ability to deal with loss of control
  - Admit it. Every CEO, including you, is a bit of a control freak. Holding onto control pushes the delegation line clockwise vs. counterclockwise.

- Willingness to buy back your own time
  - *This one is the BIG one. You CANNOT become a Green Collar CEO without the willingness to buy back your time. Every CEO says that they can't become a Green Collar CEO due to lack of capital or lack of good people, but it's a chicken or the egg issue. You can't create more value for the company bogged down in low-value tasks. If you aren't creating value, you will never have the funds to buy your way out of the very work that is holding you back. At some point, you need to place a bet on yourself. If you know you can create more value for the company, you have to buy your own time back or you will never become a Green Collar CEO.*
- LOVE
  - I hate the word "should." One of the perks of being the CEO is that the only "shoulds" are the ones you impose upon yourself. Please stop "shoulding." You are allowed to do what you LOVE. In fact, I encourage it. Who cares if the activity is below the delegation line? Do it anyway! You can't buy passion. A caveat, however: all of the activities above the delegation line don't go away while you are doing what you love. You will need to find a superstar to handle those activities in your absence.

REAL-LIFE EXAMPLE

Ron's tire store operation was a bit like firefighting. One minute there were no customers, and the next minute there were too many. Ron's long-term goal was to open additional stores, but he found it difficult to escape the firefight long enough to make the necessary arrangements. Years of being stuck wearing the Dog Collar went by before Ron sought help, but with the assistance of his coach, he realized that the daily firefight was urgent but not important, and he realized handling the daily firefight was well below his skill level. Opening additional stores was a higher value task that was not being addressed. By delegating the urgent but less important matters, Ron was able to move from the Dog Collar Delegation Line to the Blue Collar Delegation Line. Ron realized that he had to say "no" to many of the urgent activities in order to say "yes" to his new store, and he was able to open six new stores by continually pushing his delegation line toward 90°.

SOLUTION

Becoming a Green Collar CEO is not a complicated decision because all it really takes is desire, will power, and a willingness to bet on yourself. **If you really WANT to stop those low-impact activities, you will.**

You have probably figured this out already, but the Delegation Line could also be called the Entrepreneurial Line. Entrepreneurs are not willing to be bogged down with activities below their skill level or with activities that eat their precious time. This is an intricate point, and we have only scratched the surface. Be on the lookout for my next book on the details of becoming a Green Collar CEO.

NOTES:

_____

_____

_____

Fatal Error #17:
You're Right: It Isn't That Hard

Everyone knows that the business environment is changing rapidly. Are you ramping up your skills as rapidly? If your skills are stagnant, you are doing things the hard way. Many CEOs are sucked into working on the tactical aspects of the business (the "urgent" stuff), but the big money is in the strategic aspects of your business. Big strategic progress comes from new knowledge and information implemented properly.

In closely-held businesses, there are two aspects to working smart as opposed to working hard: knowledge acquisition and thought process challenge. Big businesses do a much better job at both. In big business, everyone has a boss to challenge their thinking, including the boss (who has the board of directors to answer to). Having a boss or a sounding board can keep your business decisions "on track." Without a sounding board, you run the risk of Peacock Management. Here are some examples of how to work smart as opposed to working hard:

- Attend seminars or workshops
- Join an industry group
- Benchmark
- Read one business book per month
- Join a board of directors
- Form a board of directors (note that this board must be paid or the process will fail)
- Join a CEO peer group
- Retrain yourself

REAL-LIFE EXAMPLE

For more than 20 years, Nick successfully ran his manufacturing business. When work began to move to Mexico, he weathered the storm by cutting wages, and as portions of his process began to move to Asia, Nick again reduced expenses. Nick felt it was un-American to send work overseas and prided himself on doing things the old-fashioned way.

Nick's story does not have a happy ending. Nick may have been correct to fight to keep jobs in the U.S., but he did not evolve with the manufacturing times. Nick did not implement cellular manufacturing or lean manufacturing techniques, which he referred to as "fancy MBA tricks."

Unfortunately, China does a pretty good job of "old school" manufacturing too. Nick could not compete head-to-head and was forced to shut down the business.

SOLUTION

Refocus yourself on increasing your knowledge base, your skill base, and your accountability base. Many of the options above can help you remove a "brain splinter." Have you ever tried to solve a big problem but can only seem to get a 99% effective solution? Then someone comes into your office and talks about it at length with you. During this talk, they ask you a question and the light bulb goes on over your head. You were maybe holding fast to an unwritten rule, or you maybe forgot to take something into account, or maybe you thought some potential strategy was impossible but it wasn't. In any case, your conversation partner removed a "brain splinter" for you. Another example of a "brain splinter" is when you have a key initiative that you never seem to take action on. You acknowledge its importance, and you say you are committed to action, but you don't take it. I have personally seen this situation many times. Inevitably, during a group discussion, someone brings up something the issue presenter has not thought of and the light goes on over the person's head as the brain splinter is removed. They were not moving forward on the initiative for a REASON. The brain splinter was causing doubt or uncertainty and thereby paralyzing the initiative.

Another benefit of being around a wide variety of business owners is access to creative thinking and new ideas. I have a little saying: "It is easy to think outside the box when you don't know where the box is." Business people outside your business and industry are much more capable of creative thinking about your organization because they are not constrained by industry or company convention.

Those of you opposed to reading for information, listen up. Annually, I host a webinar entitled "This Year's Top Business Books...and what you need to know about them." Go to **www.51errors.com/bookinar.html** and sign up for the next one. I will let you off the hook for not reading thousands of pages of books, but I won't let you off the hook for not knowing what the books are about or how you need to put the key points of these books into practice.

BONUS

Visit *51errors.com/books.html* for a list of recommended books useful to small business owners.

NOTES:

_____

_____

_____

_____

Fatal Error #18:
Refusing to Delegate

Yes, you are Superman or Superwoman. Yes, you can do "it" better than any of your employees. However, you run out of time at some point. J. Willard Marriott said, "Don't do ANYTHING someone else can do for you,"[7] but this seems to be the anti-creed of some business people. Their credo is, "Don't you dare let those idiots do it." The reason you don't delegate is NOT the talent level of your employees. The more likely reason you don't delegate is that you don't want to lose control. In fact, you might be complaining right now, "Things spin out of control if I delegate." CEOs who struggle to delegate effectively want to control the ACTIONS of their employees: do X, do it MY way, do it NOW, etc. I call this "chasing inputs instead of outputs." I hate to break it to you, but you can't control how your employees behave. We could spend the rest of our lives swapping war stories about the idiotic behaviors we have witnessed in our employees, but believe it or not, the root cause of these issues is not your employees.

Ironically, you have a tremendous amount of control over the people under you. If you have crummy employees, it is your fault for hiring them. Trust issues are about you again. Lousy training, your fault once more. Turnover, yep, you again.

REAL-LIFE EXAMPLE

Cindy was an extremely hard worker. She dropped out of college to start her business and had not slowed down since. Her business was wildly successful, but there are only 24 hours in a day, and Cindy ran out of hours. When she was directly involved, the business ran superbly. When she wasn't, it didn't. Cindy could never seem to find

---

7   O'Brien, Robert. *Marriott: The J. Willard Marriott Story* (Deseret Book Co., 1977), p. 266

an employee good enough to delegate important tasks to. There were no mini-Cindys running around. No one worked hard enough. No one paid enough attention to detail.

Fortunately for Cindy, or at least for the future of her business, she broke her leg skiing and was confined to the hospital for three weeks. She was FORCED to delegate. Surprisingly, Cindy's people performed pretty well without her. When Cindy was in the building, everyone knew she would "rescue" them. Therefore, her people did not perform up to their potential. It was a catch-22, but Cindy's case was fairly typical. When an owner says, "My people aren't good enough to delegate important tasks to," what she usually means is, "I am unwilling to take a chance on my people and give them permission to fail."

SOLUTION

The best managers are inherently lazy. Yes, you read that right. They have no desire to do tasks themselves. Couple this with their low tolerance for sub-standard work, and you actually have a great manager. I realize this person sounds like a mean and lazy person, but this is the make-up of many great managers. Remember "uh huh, uh huh, ignore it"? Sometimes you simply have to put up with an employee's way of doing things vs. yours in order to *not* do it yourself. Another skill excellent managers possess is understanding a condition I refer to as "they're gonna do what they're gonna do."

When you try to control the behavior of your employees, they will always disappoint you. They won't do it your way, with your speed, with your acumen, etc. Sometimes they will simply mess up or not do the task at all, but so what! You can't make them do *what* you want *how* you want it done. They are autonomous individuals entitled to make stupid choices if they so desire.

You are probably saying, "Wait a minute, Jim. You mean I have to tolerate crappy work?" No, that is not what I am saying. What I am saying is that your employees WILL give you crappy work eventually. You cannot control how they behave. However, you have to delegate tasks to them anyway.

Here is the solution: manage outputs, not inputs. Think about it. All the stuff that is driving you nuts (and causing you to avoid delegating) qualifies as INPUTS, including sloppy appearance, coming in late, not working hard enough, flirting on the job, too much cell phone use, etc. None of these infractions really matter. Do you mean to tell me that, if you had an employee who did everything that drives you nuts on the list above BUT gave you fantastic RESULTS (i.e., output), you would care? I doubt it. Typically, the employee with all the input annoyances also has poor work output, and if not, again, who cares? You are intellectually bundling. That is, you are taking two variables (poor work output plus work input annoyances) and making them ONE issue. These are two issues. Forget about the input annoyances and push the employee HARD for the output you want. By giving up on the inputs, you can actually achieve the outputs. Moreover, I think you will find that the inputs go away as well if you are getting the output. That is, if the employee is pushed to perform (output), they will not have time for the nonsense (input).

Phase two is to keep a time log of your day. What do you do with your time? Find some of the simplest work you do and delegate it. Start by delegating a part of what is on your list and keeping part, but work toward delegating all of it. Once a task has been mastered by the employee, pick another. Do NOT delegate anything new until the task is mastered. This is a common mistake. It does you no good for an employee to half-do something. Some of the factors to consider when delegating are:

- Difficulty of the task (the lower the level of difficulty, the more likely you should delegate it)
- Length of time to complete the task (the longer time the task takes, the more likely you should delegate it)

- How often does the task arise? (the more often the task arises, the more likely you should delegate it)
- How difficult is the task to train someone else to do? (the easier it is to train someone, the more likely you should delegate it)
- What is the impact on our customers if it is done wrong? (the higher impact, the less likely you should delegate it)
- How much do you like the task? (you are allowed to enjoy your day, so if you like the task, keep it)

There is a great saying: "It does not matter how well you do a task that you should not be doing." Here is one of my sayings: "Stop managing with your eyeballs." CEOs who struggle with managing the inputs vs. the outputs almost always see things that bug them: sloppy dress, goofing off, etc. Everything you see with your eyes (other than a report) is an input. If you struggle with managing with your eyeballs, work from home for two weeks. My guess is that you won't know what to do with yourself because all the busywork that arises from managing with your eyeballs is now gone.

NOTES:

_____

_____

_____

_____

Fatal Error #19:
The Cake is Flat

Baking a beautiful wedding cake requires a process and a set of ingredients. This is not unlike a business activity. When we set out to bake a cake, we follow the recipe precisely. After a while, we stop using the measuring cup and start winging it. We do the same with our business plans. When we get off the cake recipe, however, we get a flat cake. When we get off a business plan, we get "flat" business.

Everyone knows you have to have a solid business plan. How many of you have a current strategic plan? Many CEOs don't consistently work either the business or strategic plan. Why not? Sure, this is partly because they cannot see the light at the end of the tunnel. We already discussed leveraging the pyramid to help with this issue. However, many CEOs do not work their plan because they lose faith. Early on, they have a dream, but then things get bogged down in the details, which plays out as working at the bottom of the pyramid with little activity that "moves things forward." (See Error #44.)

Every CEO I have ever met is smart enough to refocus their activities and leverage their effectiveness, but most do not do it primarily because they are simply working too hard. They cannot see a way to avoid doing yet one more task.

REAL-LIFE EXAMPLE

Ryce owned a landscape company. Ryce always seemed to be bogged down in the day-to-day details of the business and eventually began to feel like she was not making the progress she should be making. After intense questioning, it became clear that Ryce had a great understanding of the overall business dynamics as well as the future direction of the industry. She foresaw the upcoming industry consolidation and could predict the shift in consumer preferences. Some of these industry "predictions" would dramatically change the business environment. If handled well, her business could be catapulted to great heights. Handled poorly, these new dynamics could put her out of business. Fortunately, Ryce's failure to work toward the coming big picture had not caused serious harm yet. However, if she continued on the same course for another two years, inroads by more forward-thinking competitors would greatly diminish her business.

Ryce understood the plan she needed to implement both tactically and strategically, but she could not break away from the day-to-day chores long enough to implement it. Ryce's business suffered eroding margins, high employee turnover, and countless headaches before the pain of not following her plan forced her to change. Fortunately, Ryce was able to work her plan and successfully re-chart the course of the business.

SOLUTION

Figure out your vision and your strategies to achieve it. If you are struggling with the vision, focus on a few key strategies to move forward. Then, find some activities to delegate, automate or stop doing altogether. For instance, I use *faqdesigner.com* to create video FAQs that substitute for the first job interview, which saves me and my partners hundreds of hours per year. If you are thinking about delegating, please do not say there is not anything that needs to be delegated or that there is no one to delegate to. This is almost always untrue. If you want to make things better, you will need to change your methods. Now, invest your newfound time in activities that drive strategic initiatives. If you do so, you will see change. The reason is simple: doing tasks only fixes problems today, but working on strategic items fixes problems permanently.

I have a philosophy: you can't move any faster pushing on the gas when the pedal is already to the floor. When I bring up planning, CEOs frequently say, "Yeah Jim, you're right. That is important. I need to do that." Okay, so the follow-up question is then: when will you do it? Face it, 100% (or more) of your time is already spoken for, and you can't push harder on the gas. You have to let go of something (see the delegation error) before you have the bandwidth to tackle anything new.

NOTES:

_____

_____

_____

_____

_____

_____

_____

Fatal Error #20:
Are You Bobby Fischer or Bobby Riggs?

Some CEOs can inherently manage multiple tasks, priorities, and contingencies. Others inherently think very linearly and can only see a couple moves ahead. Running a business is a lot like a game of chess. The further ahead you can anticipate the direction your sector will move or your competitors will turn, the better player you are. A novice chess player may only be thinking one or two moves ahead. Masterful chess players think seven or more moves ahead. In business, these moves ahead are typically contingencies, forks in the road, or unanticipated problems. The successful CEOs have already anticipated the issues and are fully prepared to deal with them.

If you do not run your business like a champion chess player, you are closer to Bobby Riggs than Bobby Fischer. Bobby Fischer was a world champion chess player. Bobby Riggs challenged Billy Jean King to the first male/female tennis match and was humiliated on national television. Evidently, Mr. Riggs failed to anticipate only one move ahead (that he might lose).

REAL-LIFE EXAMPLE

Larry Linear is the CEO of Linear Technologies. Linear's lease is due to expire in six months. Larry would like to move and purchase a building. Larry's quick read on the problem is as follows: 1) locate a new space, 2) notify the landlord he is not renewing the lease, 3) move. This sequence seems simple and straightforward enough. However, after Larry falls in love with a new building, another buyer outbids him. Now Larry is four months from the move. He now goes to his second option. After a week of hunting down the seller, he finds out that the seller has decided to stay in the building. None of the other options are attractive to Larry, so he scrambles to look for rentable space. Larry cannot finalize a lease in time, and so he is forced to renew with his current landlord at the eleventh hour. The landlord knows Larry's predicament and raises the rent.

In a similar scenario, Curt Concurrent, CEO of Concurrent Electric, pursued many options at once. He started negotiating with the landlord six months prior to lease expiration so he could not be held over the barrel. He made offers on several pieces of property, even ones he was not excited about. In the end, his first option did not work out, but he was able to move because he was running multiple scenarios simultaneously. His first option did not work, but he still accomplished his goal.

SOLUTION

Bobby Riggs-type thinkers don't run the B and C scenarios UNTIL the A scenario fails. They think sequentially and linearly vs. running parallel options through their minds at the same time, a recipe for failure. Business always has delays and unexpected events. Much of a plan is "hurry up and wait," but while you are waiting, be pursuing multiple options. Do not discard an option until you are SURE the other option is locked-in.

This error is not meant to be a justification for all of you over-jugglers. You know who you are. You are always trying to manage fifteen priorities instead of five. Sequential thinkers get "stuck." Over-jugglers are busy, active, and productive but never finish anything. They spend all their time moving lots of action items forward. Unfortunately, the benefits of the work do not accrue because half-finished work typically has little value.

Fatal Error #21:
"Field of Dreams" Thinking

"If you build it, they will come" works well for big businesses because they are not nimble enough to start small and adjust quickly, and so they have to build it first and build it big. Small businesses, however, should first conceive it, then create basic marketing materials, then test their ability to sell it, then scramble to build it.

REAL-LIFE EXAMPLE

Ramon started his technology business to capitalize on an emerging mobile technology. Ramon spent $5,000 for a Gartner Research report predicting the growth of the segment. He spent tens of thousands of dollars attending trade shows to learn more about the industry leaders. Most importantly, Ramon recruited a rising star from G.E. to head up the technical side of the business. Ramon even gave this star 25% of the company stock. Ramon spent the bulk of the first six months in business forging strategic alliances that would be needed as rapid growth ensued. You can probably guess the rest. Sales never came. The industry grew at 10% annually, not the 125% predicted. The technology was adopted much slower than expected, and the business folded when Ramon's seed capital was exhausted.

SOLUTION

Being well prepared is important, but remember what Tom Peters says: "Ready, Fire, Aim."[8] In other words, Peters is promoting experimentation followed by preparation, rather than lots of preparation followed by action, or "Ready, Aim, Aim, Aim, Aim, Fire."

---

8   Peters, Tom & Waterman, Robert. *In Search of Excellence* (HarperCollins, 1982), p.119

Stop being so afraid to fail. It is our JOB as entrepreneurs to fail. You've heard it before: "Fail faster." Now go out there and do it. A caveat though: fail as cheaply as possible. Fast failure IS cheaper.

NOTES:

_____

_____

_____

_____

_____

_____

_____

_____

_____

_____

Fatal Error #22:
Chopping Your Own Wood

E ntrepreneurs tend to have a pioneer mentality. Entrepreneurs clear the trees for their homestead. They chop their own wood and build their own cabins with their own two hands. They plow the fields and plant the crops for the food they eat. Shoot, we entrepreneurs are practically Martha Stewart molding the pottery to plant our rhubarb for the pie we will make two months from now.

Entrepreneurs who want to do it all by themselves feel less than adequate when they seek help. "Help" is a four-letter word to these entrepreneurs, but in truth, the best entrepreneurs have a tinge of laziness in their character that enables them to delegate low-impact tasks. This helpful laziness causes them to "find someone else to do it." Many times, this someone else has more expertise than the entrepreneur and therefore brings something extra to the business. Many times, this extra expertise translates into a strategic advantage for the business.

REAL-LIFE EXAMPLE

Ken's LAN/WAN business was in a tough marketplace. New competitors were popping up weekly, margins were under pressure, and Ken's arch-rival, Sam, had a virtually identical business. They had the same number of employees and the same sales volume. Ken felt he needed a leg-up on Sam, so he hired a consultant to re-tool his sales process. By the end of the year, Ken's sales were double Sam's. Ken complained that the consulting project was expensive, but he admitted that the cost of a stagnant business was more expensive.

SOLUTION

Treat expert intellectual property like you would treat an investment in a machine. Investments pay returns. If you calculate the rate of return for the purchase of a machine, also calculate the rate of return for intellectual property/advice. An investment in a tangible item such as a machine makes us feel more comfortable than buying ideas. Sometimes, ideas don't work, but the best case return for expert intellectual property purchases yield returns no machine can match.

NOTES:

_____

_____

_____

_____

_____

_____

_____

_____

_____

_____

Fatal Error #23:
Leave Me Alone

Owning a business is a lonely job. There's a lot of stress and not many ways to get support. You cannot talk to your employees, who will hold what you tell them against you. Your family cares about you, but they don't really understand. Many of your friends and neighbors are not in business for themselves. Here is the rub: Help is a 4-LETTER word to a business owner, and getting a coach or a peer group seems too much like help. We entrepreneurs would much rather create a company that nets a million dollars independently than create a company that nets ten million dollars with help. I don't know if it is pride, ego, stubbornness, or all of the above that prevents us from thus succeeding by simply seeking input.

REAL-LIFE EXAMPLE

Rudy had owned his service firm for many years. Over that time, Rudy had rescued Irv from his failing business and made him the "right-hand man." Rudy continued to hand more responsibility to Irv until Rudy felt Irv was an equal partner in the business. When Rudy returned from his vacation, he learned Irv had raided the customer files, erased computers, and met with all the customers asking them to migrate to Irv's new firm. Rudy felt like throwing in the towel. With the support of his CEO group, Rudy was able to weather the storm emotionally. This traumatic event actually was the impetus for Rudy to take his business to the next level. Today, Rudy's business is in a significantly better position than before.

SOLUTION

The qualities of ego, stubbornness, and pride that cause us *not* to seek needed assistance also aid us in being highly entrepreneurial. You must find a way to keep these excellent qualities when needed and discard them when they are not serving you. Harv Eker, author of *Secrets of the Millionaire Mind,* has a great saying: "You can be RICH, or you can be RIGHT."

One of my CEO group members says, "Who is your priest?" Every business owner needs someone they can confide in, complain to, consult with, and with whom they can brainstorm. Find someone who can do this for you. Find a group of business owners who can help you with support and advice.

NOTES:

_____

_____

_____

_____

_____

_____

_____

_____

_____

_____

CHAPTER 4

Best and Worst Practices

I am a lucky guy. I get to travel the country and speak to thousands of different business owners. I get to sit down with some of them one-on-one and learn their success secrets. Unfortunately, there is no real school you can attend to teach you to be in business. As noted previously, the most effective school is the School of Hard Knocks, but attendance is expensive and slow. If you have ever hired a poor salesperson and hung on to them too long, ask yourself how much the class called "When to Know When You Need to Fire a Worthless Salesperson" cost you? Most entrepreneurs have paid $50,000-$100,000+ for this course at the School of Hard Knocks.

Gleaning best practices that work for other businesses and adapting them is one of the best ways to circumvent the School of Hard Knocks. The following errors represent some of the best practices I have observed over the past 25 years. Please keep a very open mind when you read them. While reading them, if you say to yourself, "Yeah, that might work in the XYZ business, but I make computer parts," you are losing all the potential benefits. I am 100% confident that 100% of these best practices CAN be applied to your business. I have spoken with executives at Fortune 500 companies who have told me that these errors are equally applicable in a large company setting. The key is keeping an open mind and reading them with a positive expectation.

NOTES:

_____

_____

_____

_____

_____

_____

_____

_____

_____

_____

_____

Fatal Error #24:
Hiring Bargain-Basement Help

As everyone knows, you get what you pay for, but few of us operate that way. Yet more ironically, few businesses follow the rule "the systems run the business, the people run the systems." Without good systems, better people are required. Yet it is these same operators that want to buy their help at the flea market.

You cannot expect talented employees to work for below average wages. However, because many CEOs have occasionally gotten a bargain on an excellent employee, they make their pay strategy the "bargain basement" strategy (see "Treating Exceptions as the Rule", Error #5). This intermittent reinforcement has led them to believe that it is possible to get good people cheaply. They also have overpaid bad people, so they feel like they are wasting money paying *anyone* more. This downward spiral starts at recruitment. You cannot recruit great people for low dough.

REAL-LIFE EXAMPLE

Sally prided herself on her bargain hunting ability, a practice that spilled over into her employment searches. When Sally needed an administrator, she thought to herself, "This is an easy job. It doesn't really require much more than a glorified clerk." Sally figured she could get a good person for $8 per hour. Sally did find a "qualified" person for $8 per hour. Training the new administrator took a bit longer than Sally figured, but hey, she was getting a $12 per hour person for $8 per hour. Over time, the administrator became an important resource for Sally, but her attendance became spotty. Sally was frustrated that, whenever she needed the administrator the most, she missed work. You've never wore that Dog Collar, right?

Sally felt like firing her administrator, but how could she find someone else for only $8 per hour. Therefore she tolerated the spotty attendance. Eventually, the admin took a job for $12 per hour at another firm. Sally was forced to raise the pay of the position and retrain a new person.

SOLUTION

There are several ways to mess things up in this regard: 1) pay less than the market rate for the position, 2) pay a good person less than they are worth to the company, 3) slot moderately qualified people into moderately underpaid positions.

The downsides are as follows: 1) you better have great training because you are starting with lower caliber people; 2) if you do not pay market rate for good people, you will only get those willing to work for less (a.k.a. the bad ones); if you fill your business with mediocre performers, good performers will not want to work for you — winners attract winners; 3) you will spend a tremendous amount of energy training mediocre people and turning them into good performers only to have them leave for more money — you will be relegated to being a "farm team" for other companies; 4) most importantly, your time is the most valuable time in the organization and your time is being wasted by poor people. Simply don't tolerate it. **Your business can only move at the speed you move.** Anchoring yourself down with poor people hinders your ability to make your business something special.

For the next phase, rate your existing staff. You probably have some poor performers. Start the upgrade process. You will need to replace your poor performers with better ones. Pay what you need to pay to get the talent you need. Don't pay your existing people more. You are already paying them enough to *not* quit, so don't waste your money on them. Use your limited funds to find better talent. You will most likely be able to reduce headcount with better-quality people. One terrific employee can do the work of two or three poor ones.

If you are guilty of being chintzy on your payroll, you are "tap-dancing on the landmines," and you will blow up if you slip up. Businesses are held together by quality people. If you are being cheap with your help, you don't have a lot of quality people. All it takes is a couple of them to quit and you have a BIG problem.

NOTES:

_____

_____

_____

_____

_____

_____

_____

_____

_____

Fatal Error #25:
Fire Slowly, Hire Quickly

Wait Jim, don't you mean hire slowly, fire quickly? Nope. I got it right. These are business ERRORS after all. Poor training and systems are the root cause of the reverse strategy, causing us to hire from our gut and give bad employees too many chances. Your business is made up of human capital. There is this part of me that is REALLY resentful of this fact. I spend all my time, energy, talents, time, and capital building a great business, and its future, my future, is in the hands of my "human capital." That sucks! Whether it sucks or not, however, it is reality. The higher the quality of your people, the better your business. Holding a spot for a sub-standard performer has opportunity costs. How much better would your business be if you traded all your bad performers for superstars? Building your business team is not unlike fielding a baseball team. Sometimes you need to trade players.

REAL-LIFE EXAMPLE

Dan was the type of interviewer who tended to fall in love with a candidate. Dan would effectively make up his mind to hire someone five minutes into the interview. All future interviewees had little chance to win the job. One time, Dan so loved the first candidate that he hired her on the spot and cancelled all future interviews. Unfortunately for Dan, his instincts were not always correct. Some of the candidates were a testament to the adage "what are all employees best at: selling themselves." These employees were not good at much else.

Dan liked his people, and he truly cared about them. He knew they had kids and bills to pay. When Dan thought about terminating some-one, he asked himself, "How will they pay their bills if they don't have a job?" Once an employee finally was terminated, however, Dan frequently found himself saying, "I wish I would have gotten rid of that person a year ago." Dan found his personality got in the way of doing what was right.

He enlisted the help of his CEO group. He asked them to hold him accountable. If he consistently complained about an employee, the group was to start an impromptu conversation regarding the person's termination, resulting in a resolution acceptable to the group — accountability was created for Dan. This "positive trap" helped Dan take the necessary action.

SOLUTION

Your personality may be a hindrance to textbook management. If so, create a trap to force yourself to do what is needed. **Yours is not the only company with available employment.** Your people managed to survive prior to their employment with you, and they will survive afterward. Many times it is better for the employee to seek another opportunity rather than remaining in a job where they are failing.

Like or dislike George Steinbrenner, he gets this right. He took a terrible New York Yankee organization in the early 1970s and turned it into a money machine. Part of Steinbrenner's success formula was to always upgrade. A player could win the MVP this year and be out of a job next year if Steinbrenner found someone better.

Fatal Error #26:
Turning Racehorses into Plow Horses

Keeping good people in areas that are critical to your business is never easy, and this task may even make it harder for you. This title is designed to make you visualize a sleek, tall, and strong horse tied to a plow. Of course a horse is a horse, and the racehorse is certainly capable of pulling the plow, but the real question is this: is there a more critical task that they could be doing to be even more valuable to the organization?

Think back to the Delegation Grid discussed earlier in the book. Your racehorses should be plugged into those areas that are just below YOUR delegation line. People who are dedicated and value-driven will do whatever you need them to do. Even if you don't or can't calculate the opportunity cost of having them performing jobs that they are over qualified for, consider the following. When talented and driven people are assigned to tasks that do not challenge them, one of two things happens:

1. They become bored with the work and their frustration leads to them leaving the organization. Now not only have you lost a talented racehorse, but the plow is now sitting on the field going nowhere. Each of these facts has a cost, and depending on the size of your company, the next horse to pull the plow may be you!

2. They become so disillusioned that they grow apathetic and can even become rebellious and cause issues at work as their performance slips. The fields are not being plowed correctly, the rows are running with the grade of the hill, and yields are down. I will suggest that this option is much worse than the first, as they are now infecting others in the organization and can be a cancer eating away at your culture and profits.

REAL WORLD EXAMPLE

Ed was running a sizable logistics company and had put a person in a job who was not performing at the level needed. Ed realized that he had asked a plow horse to run in the derby and that this horse was being clocked with a calendar instead of a watch. The company was paying too high a cost to keep this person in this position. Ed felt that he did not have anyone on his current team who could handle the position, so he needed to go outside of the company to HIRE an expert. Once the new racehorse was located and hired, Ed had to have a heart-to-heart with his plow horse and ask him to step down from that position so that the new guy could start the job. As you might guess, that talk didn't go well, and the person he asked to step down resigned. That was not at all what Ed wanted as he liked the person and knew he could contribute in other ways.

Well, the situation got even worse as the next week another person in the division resigned as well because this person felt they had been overlooked for the new job. They said they had been quietly performing these tasks (pulling the plow) for a long time just waiting for the opportunity to advance. As you can imagine, here was Ed losing two great people and having to work IN his business until they could be replaced and the new person could learn the process.

SOLUTION

There is no magic wand, but I implore each of you to work at developing and nurturing a culture wherein people feel free to ask for more responsibility without fear of being seen as selfish. You want and need people who want to grow, and you want to keep them around as long as possible.

Watch for people who are frustrated. Frustration is a key point of pain for people who are not feeling satisfaction from their work. Frustration is often made evident in attitude.

- Use tools to ensure you know the needs and motivations as well as the talents of your players.
- Communicate with your employees often, and ask them what they want. Ask them what their goals are and where they envision themselves in two to five years (SILENCE is not acceptance). This is especially true for people who have been with you for over a year and do good work.
- Watch for people who are becoming rebels because this is a shift in their actions that is a key indicator of dissatisfaction.
- Know what skills and personality traits are critical to a position before moving someone into the job. Move slowly. Do not make another error by making a quick decision that has to be reversed later.

NOTES:

_____

_____

_____

_____

_____

_____

_____

_____

Fatal Error #27:
Do They Graduate or Quit?

You have to decide what kind of company you want yours to be. When it comes to employees, there are only two kinds of companies: those who graduate their employees and those whose employees quit. This is a bit of forced polarization because it ignores the steady mass of employees in the middle, but that said, the steady masses are not what make your company succeed or fail. The superstars, or lack of them, will most likely determine your company's level of success.

Companies with great training tend to graduate employees, and companies with poor or non-existent training tend to have employees quit. My instinct is that owners are reluctant to "graduate" their employees because they don't want to lose someone who is a superstar. So they don't train them and give them a chance to be a superstar and the employee quits. This company is denied the benefit of having the superstar on staff for all the time prior to when they would have graduated. The large accounting firms are great at avoiding this. They train and train and train their new people, and most of them are gone to greener pastures in only two years, but the accounting firm gets the benefit of hardworking, bright employees for a bargain price for two years. The brightest business students in the country seek out jobs at the large firms because they know that two years of paying dues will yield them a better job.

Most businesses complain that their people are not loyal, but I see far too many businesses that won't spend $100 to send someone to Excel training or a management seminar. Sending your good people to formal training tells them, "You are important around here."

Everyone has seen the data: money is seventh on the list of employee motivators. Many times, we dismiss this fact, however. If the employee views the pay as adequate or better than adequate (this does not mean they won't complain about money, of course), then money really is seventh on the motivation list. If the money is inadequate, however, money is first, second, *and* third.

If money is far down the list of motivators, what DOES motivate employees? Many of the factors above money have to do with the "quality" of the job. What makes a job high quality? The list includes a solid promotion path and the ability to be promoted to their level of incompetence.

How does an employee get promoted and grow? Training plays a huge role. Employees need to sharpen their saws too. If you withhold training, you are capping their career, and they will eventually figure this out. The good employees will leave and only the bad ones will stay.

REAL-LIFE EXAMPLE

Sarah was elated when she was able to out-recruit the big firms and hire Ann, who was supremely talented and capable of taking Sarah's company to the next level. However, Sarah put all her energy into recruiting Ann and none of her energy into retaining her. Ann, like all quality employees, had mentioned during interviews that improving her computer skills was a priority. Sarah felt ill equipped to train Ann, so she ignored the request. Eventually, Ann quit, citing a variety of reasons. The real, and unmentioned, reason Ann quit was that she felt her progress was being slowed by lack of training and additional responsibility. By investing in a few computer or management training courses, Sarah could have avoided this costly error.

SOLUTION

Create a budget for seminars and training. Consider creating in-house training programs. Realize that training is a valid way to recruit and retain great employees.

BONUS

Visit *51errors.com/invest.html* for example programs how to invest in your people.

Fatal Error #28:
Ignoring Your Best Performers

Sometimes we are so busy trying to grow that we forget the people who got us where we are. Don't ignore your stars. If you ignore them too long, they will go somewhere where they are appreciated.

Every business owner out there has experienced this scenario: an employee with key knowledge walks into your office and says, "I love you and I love working for you, but I have an offer I just can't refuse." Most of the time, the CEO finds extra money or whatever else is necessary to retain the employee. My suggestion is to be proactive about keeping your key people rather than finding yourself in this position.

REAL-LIFE EXAMPLE

Yolanda's business was growing rapidly. Like most business owners, she was an excellent problem solver. One key to Yolanda's success was Rachel, employee #1 for the company. Rachel was Yolanda's right-hand person. Over time, Rachel was given several raises and was making an excellent wage. However, Yolanda was so busy growing the business that Rachel was rarely praised for her heroics, and despite Rachel's significant pay raises, her job responsibilities had stayed constant. Much to Yolanda's surprise, Rachel quit. Yolanda tried to give Rachel another raise, but it was too late. Rachel had found a position for less money but that included more skill growth and responsibility.

SOLUTION

Paying attention to your key employees goes a long way. "Pay" is more money to an employee. A raise is a way of saying, "You are valuable around here and I appreciate you." Ask yourself, "If this person quit, how much grief would it cause?" If it is a lot of grief, ask yourself, "How much would I pay them to stay?" Now, give that key employee one-fourth of the raise you would give them in the "I'm quitting" scenario. Trust me. I just saved you a ton of money and grief. Repeat the process for all key employees. If money is tight, give the raises one at a time or as cash allows.

Give your stars an unexpected day off or tickets to the movies or just an attaboy. There are many ways to reward employees, and there are many books written on the subject of employee rewards. For example, as a good starting point, try *24 Carrot Manager* by Adrian Gostick.

If you are like most business owners, you have had the thought, "Forget that attaboy-group-hug junk. I already pay them enough. I am a good boss and I treat them well." I hear you loud and clear. You are not nuts or wrong in your thinking. Most owners feel this way some or all the time. Now shut that voice off and read this point over again because you are about to make a mess. Thank you.

NOTES:

_____

_____

_____

_____

_____

Fatal Error #29: Ignoring Your Worst Performers

I don't know if I subscribe to the Jack Welch philosophy, "fire your worst 10% every year," but most small businesses keep the losers far too long. For all the tough-guy CEO bravado, many CEOs are wimps when it comes to getting rid of the dead weight.

My theory is that many CEOs avoid firing poor employees to avoid the fallout, the extra work, the training, and the headaches they will have to endure after the firing. However, they have simply chosen to perpetuate the pain, chosen death by a thousand cuts, as it were, rather than enduring a single short, deep cut. I can hear your complaints already? "I can't find anyone good to replace them. That employee knows too much about the business to be replaced." Instead of enduring the one-time pain of the deep cut, some CEOs choose to "boil the frog," to change the metaphor up a bit. You can boil a frog to death by slowly heating the water. The frog has the ability to jump out of the water, but the change is "only a little worse," so the frog stays in the pot and boils to death. Guess who is the frog in this analogy? You are! Don't be a frog!

REAL-LIFE EXAMPLE

Mark was scrambling to hire another ten employees for his restaurant. During a conversation, Mark mentioned he had three employees who were "worthless." I asked him why they still worked for him, and Mark responded, "I can't replace them with anyone better, so I put up with them." There is a distinct difference between a "slot-filler" and a poor employee. Mark eventually discovered that poor performers need to be rehabilitated, retrained, or replaced, and his business ran much better once he maintained this philosophy.

SOLUTION

Slot-fillers are fine until you find someone better. Just put your efforts into replacing them instead of complaining about them. The root of this problem is in the business systems you have in place, not in the employee. In particular, the training systems are problematic in such instances. If you are afraid of turnover, you probably try to buy skill instead of building it. True, skill/talent is in short supply, but invest in training systems, and in a few years you won't have turnover issues or need to buy talent.

Stop complaining about your bad performers and force yourself to pay $50.00 each time you complain about someone who needs to be fired. This act will break you of the habit. **For a problem employee, follow the three R's: rehabilitate them, retrain them, or rid yourself of them.**

If you can't figure out whether or not an employee is dead weight, use what I call a "commitment test." A commitment test is a pre-designed fork in the road. You don't care which way they go; you just want to see which way they pick. For instance, if you question your employee's loyalty, have a mandatory Saturday work day. The loyal ones will show up and the non-loyal ones won't.

Here is another acid test to spot troublesome employees. I call it the "trip to the money tree test." Have your employees ever said something or acted like this?

Every Friday, the boss lets me through the gate they guard to pick some bills from the money tree. I really wish the boss would stop being so stingy and let me pluck a few

more bills from the tree. After all, there is this whole tree full of money.

Every business owner has felt this way about an employee, that they see no correlation between their work and their pay. The employee in this example has an entitlement mentality. You need employees who understand that they are paid in direct proportion to the value they create for the business. They are in complete control of their pay, not you. What the employee in this example wants is for you to take responsibility for their productivity and pay them for more than they create.

NOTES:

_____

_____

_____

_____

_____

_____

_____

_____

Fatal Error #30:
1924 Management Techniques
are Still Valid

The Hawthorne effect describes a temporary change of behavior or performance due to a change in the environmental conditions. This change is typically an improvement, a.k.a. motivation. The term gets its name from a factory called the *Hawthorne Works*, where a series of experiments on factory workers was carried out between 1924 and 1932.[9]

Many types of experiments were conducted on the employees, but the purpose of the original experiments was to study the effect of lighting on worker productivity. Researchers found that productivity almost always increased after a change in illumination, but later productivity returned to normal levels. This effect was observed for even minute increases in illumination.

These studies were the humble beginning of what is now termed organizational behavior. Organizational behavior is the psychology of the workplace. In 1959, behavioral psychologist Frederick Hertzberg discovered what he called hygiene factors,[10] which are demotivators in the workplace. Examples might include everything from incomprehensible compensation systems, a dirty workplace, never having coffee filters, a noisy work environment, or a million other annoyances. Organizational behavior studies have shown that removal of hygiene factors does NOT, repeat NOT, motivate employees. That is, getting the secretary the fax machine she asked for does NOT motivate her, but it stops the demotivation. Most managers do not understand this dynamic and treat employees like they should be grateful for the removal of the hygiene factor.

---

9 www.en.wikipedia.org/wiki/Hawthorne_effect
10 Herzberg, Frederick. *The Motivation to Work* (New York: John Wiley and Sons, 1959)

Most mangers also do a lousy job of searching out hygiene factors and rectifying them. They may view the factor as merely an employee complaining or simply as an annoyance. Allowing hygiene factors in the workplace lowers productivity and is a known cause of turnover. Many hygiene factors are simple and inexpensive to rectify.

REAL-LIFE EXAMPLE

Ira had a reputation as a demanding boss, but Ira was also inspiring. Ira had inspired tremendous loyalty in his key people. This loyalty was tested over time as office space grew cramped, broken copiers were fixed rather than replaced, and requests for needed upgrades were denied. Ira's business had been very profitable for fifteen years, but this year was very soft, break-even at best. One day, Ira's key people called an impromptu "meeting," which Ira considered more of an ambush. His key people effectively demanded more office space and better working conditions, and Ira could not afford to fire them. First of all, they were right. Conditions were unacceptable. Second, he could not replace all his key people at once. Ira was forced to spend money he did not have upgrading systems and equipment all at once when he could have been taking the necessary steps one at a time if he had been sensitive to these hygiene issues previously.

SOLUTION

Have your employees complete a blind survey. It is imperative that the employees remain anonymous. If an employee can be singled out, the good suggestions will never be mentioned. You can also use a third party, like a consultant, to hold a group meeting (without you present) to discuss hygiene improvements. A caveat: if you ask for a list of hygiene factors, you MUST take action on some of them. You do not need to fix all of them, but if you do not rectify some of them, you will make the situation worse. You will be effectively communicating to your employees, "Yes, I know we have issues that make your job stink, but I don't care."

BONUS

Visit *51errors.com/hygiene.html* for a list of common hygiene issues as well as additional information.

NOTES:

Fatal Error #31:
Two Out of Three Ain't Bad

One of every manager's biggest frustrations is motivating employees. There are dozens of theories on motivation, but one of the best is the theory of Expectancy,[11] and the tenets are as follows:

- There must be an effort/performance linkage (How hard will I have to work?)
- There must be a performance/reward linkage (What is the reward?)
- There must be attractiveness (How attractive is the reward?)

I would argue that all plans to effectively motivate employees must take all three of the above factors into account. If you only have two tenets of Expectancy Theory in effect, it won't work at ALL. In the world of motivation, two out of three gets you nothing. If you analyze an employee's lack of motivation through the lens of Expectancy Theory, you can almost always find a missing link.

Many times, managers project their own standards on employees. For instance, the effort/performance linkage refers to the employee's subjective opinion, which is sometimes askew. *Your* opinion of how much effort a given task will take is completely irrelevant. When we project our opinions and standards onto employees, Expectancy Theory fails to work. That is, "I like cash so they must like cash too." The best managers project no opinions on what should motivate their people, which allows the employees to craft motivational incentives based upon what they desire without subjective judgment regarding the value of the incentive.

---

11 Green, Thad B. *Performance and Motivation Strategies for Today's Workforce: A Guide to Expectancy Theory Applications* (Quorum Books, 1992), p.10

REAL-LIFE EXAMPLE

Jean was elated with her new sales contest. The winner of the sales contest would win a two day, all expenses paid trip for two to a far-away spa. Jean was almost envious she could not win the prize herself. At the end of the contest, however, Jean was disappointed that sales for many of the employees were flat. Jean picked a prize she wanted, not one the employees wanted. Several of the salespeople had small children, so extended travel was complicated. Some of the employees were not "spa people." Jean wasted her money to motivate one or two salespeople who did value the prize.

SOLUTION

Many books about motivation are available. One of the best is Frank McNair's *It's OK to Ask 'Em to Work*.[12] One of the best pieces of advice you will read therein is don't do contests just for the sake of doing contests. Some companies always have a sales contest underway. The most powerful form of reinforcement (i.e., motivation) is intermittent reinforcement, and continual contests are obviously not intermittent reinforcement and have fleeting motivational value.

Remember, check your personal opinions at the door when you are motivating your employees. Some of the most successful motivational prizes I personally considered "stupid," which only proves that I don't know what I don't know (what will motivate employees at any given time in a given context). My personal favorite motivational "carrot" was when a client was going to give a day off to his entire staff during

---

12 McNail, Frank. *It's OK to Ask 'Em to Work...and Other Essential Maxims for Smart Managers* (New York: American Management Association, 2000)

slow season. Instead of just giving it to them, he created a goal for them. If they achieved the goal, they got the day off he was planning to give them anyway. Now that's an inexpensive incentive!

NOTES:

_____

_____

_____

_____

_____

_____

_____

_____

_____

_____

_____

_____

Fatal Error #32: Whiff-em Has Nothing to Do with Baseball

Whiff-em (or WIIFM) is short for "what's in it for me." Basic economic principles state that everyone is acting in their own economic self-interest at ALL times. This is not as Machiavellian as it might sound, but reality. Look at the issues and motivations from the employees' view, and you will become a better manager.

Projecting your personal values onto others can be very dangerous. You will struggle to deal with vendors, customers and employees because you will never see things from their point of view. You will end up with a company of "mini-me's" if you project. That is, only those motivated by what motivates you will want to work the incentives. If this is the case, you will lose the value of diversity. I am not only talking about social, racial, and economic diversity, but about HUMAN DIVERSITY. Differences in employee personalities and motivation make organizations stronger if the organization knows how to harness the power of this diversity. If you do not know how to harness it, diversity becomes a pain in the rear and the power is lost.

REAL-LIFE EXAMPLE

Mac desperately needed some publicity. His business was struggling and needed some exposure to push things over the top. Mac called every newspaper in town to run a story on his clothing store, but what was the WIIFM for the newspaper editor? Why run a story on just another clothing store? What interest would their readers have? Mac was not an advertiser, so it would not be an obligatory piece for the paper. During his coaching session, Mac realized the issues and took corrective action. He wrote a "spec" piece on his business (WIIFM = no need for the paper to write an article because it's already done).

He pitched the editor on a unique aspect of his business that could be helpful to the editor's readership. Through a variety of WIIFM changes, Mac was able to secure an abundance of PR.

SOLUTION

When you assume what someone else wants, you are "throwing darts blindfolded," trying to hit a target that you cannot see. Eventually, you may hit the target by accident, but you will just create an expensive mess before you do.

Again, check your personal opinions and values at the door. Managing people is a role you play. It is not you. You are ACTING. You are not acting in a devious or evil way. You are acting to play the role of the best manager on the planet. Unfortunately, you playing yourself is probably not the best manager on the planet. Therefore, you have to act.

NOTES:

_____

_____

_____

_____

_____

_____

_____

Fatal Error #33:
Not Invented Here Syndrome

In 1899, Charles H. Duell, the Commissioner of the U.S. Patent Office, said, "Everything that can be invented has been invented." He advocated closing the patent office. Is your patent office closing? Is your mind closed to new, fresh, unique or different ideas? Typically, the longer a CEO is in business, the more averse to new ideas they become. Just because you did not think of an idea doesn't mean it won't work, it isn't any good, or you can come up with a better idea.

REAL-LIFE EXAMPLE

It was our lucky day. Our association got an opportunity to tour the plant belonging to one of our client's big competitors. We took copious notes, and we noted several improvement opportunities for our client, but when we sat down to share our thoughts, the client was less than enthusiastic. We heard, "I don't want to do anything XYZ is doing — they don't have a clue about this market." Our client was blinded by the source of these good ideas, but good ideas are good ideas. Do not concern yourself with the source.

SOLUTION

Ask your people for three ideas each. Whereas Americans tend to swing for the fences all the time, I suggest you follow the lead of the Japanese: no idea is too small. I'll bet you will get dozens of great ideas. You can also borrow ideas from your competition, which Tom Peters calls "creative swiping." There are great ideas all around; use them.

Honestly answer this question: Is it more important to be able to say, "Look how great my idea worked out" or to be able to say, "Look what I accomplished using someone else's idea"? Which source of pride feels better to you?

NOTES:

_____

_____

_____

_____

_____

_____

_____

_____

_____

Fatal Error #34:
Being Too Busy "Doing the Work"

f this cartoon reminds you of someone, I hope it isn't yourself. I like to call this syndrome "Stop bothering me for I am too busy chasing my tail in a circle to stop chasing my tail in a circle."

"Stop bothering me, I'm busy"

This issue is akin to "working *in* your business, not *on* it." Doing "the work" is sometimes good. "The work" is the day-to-day activities of your business, but many CEOs wonder, "What will I do if I don't do the work?" Importantly, these CEOs are also fond of saying, "I can't afford to delegate the work." The answer is simple. Your business will not grow meaningfully with you doing *the work*. If you are doing the day-to-day work, you are the bottleneck. Do you think Donald Trump is dealing cards at the blackjack table?

REAL-LIFE EXAMPLE

After Greta had worked for a major real estate firm for 20 years, she launched her own property management company and worked long hours to keep her clients happy. Greta would wake up at 4 a.m. to ensure parking lots were plowed. She personally oversaw accounting issues. She met with clients regularly. Every time her coach wanted to talk about strategic initiatives or long-term goals, Greta would say, "I simply don't have time for that." Three years after launching her business, she was making more money on her own than she had from her previous job. However, the hours were demanding for a single mother. Then the other shoe dropped. A new competitor entered the market offering free services for a year, effectively stealing many of Greta's customers but also making it virtually impossible to attract new business. Each coaching session, Greta would complain about the competitor, but she made no structural changes to her business model. She simply "did not have time." After a very long, tough year, Greta slowed down enough to look at her business strategically. With the help of her coach, she re-tooled her business model. Now she is attracting new business and is far less harried.

SOLUTION

Monitor how you spend your time for a week or two, and then categorize where you spent your time. If most activities only "keep things going," you are selling yourself short. As the CEO, you are responsible for the "big stuff." If you eat up your calendar on the "little stuff," you won't have the energy or hours to move your business forward.

Be willing to "buy back your own time." Many CEOs complain, "I can't afford to delegate what I do to someone else, and this is typically a fair assessment. However, the CEO is trapped. If she cannot offload the work, she cannot move on to higher impact activities and the business will move forward slowly, if at all. You must have the courage to bet on your yourself. Buy back some of your time.

Let's make a little bet. Keep an honest and accurate time log for a month. Add up the hours on the strategic activities. If you can look back at your business activities this month five years from now and say, "I am SO glad I spent my time doing that," the activity in question is strategic. If you can't say that, it's just "work." Now, here's the bet: I'll bet you are spending less than 20 hours a month on strategic items, and in fact, I'll bet that some of you are spending less than 10 hours per month on strategic items. That is the bad news. The good news is: think of your upside!

NOTES:

_____

_____

_____

_____

_____

_____

Fatal Error #35:
Pay No Attention to the Man
Behind the Curtain

I know I just told you to avoid the busywork, but hand signing checks and reviewing bank statements are tasks that fall above the delegation line (Fatal Error #16). Such tasks only take a small amount of time, but doing these tasks could save you hundreds of thousands of dollars.

Many CEOs do not enjoy accounting, so they abdicate the function. Here is a list of embezzlement scams I know of firsthand:

- Employee buying a car on the company American Express card and paying for it in full before being discovered.
- Employee obtaining PIN numbers on several company cards and getting thousands of dollars in cash advances.
- Controller "borrowing" company funds to purchase nine Holiday Inn franchises over a several year period. In this case, the employee paid back 100% of the money. When the company was audited, he was caught within hours.
- Controller going "nuts" on the job. His instructions were to "get payables more under control." So he drew down the remaining $105,000 on the company line without permission, paid the funds to creditors as well as writing checks for $100,000 more than the cash in the bank. The owner found his bank account overdrawn by $100,000, had hundreds of bounced checks that amounted to $10,000 in bounced-check FEES, and his payroll was due in two days.

REAL-LIFE EXAMPLE

Tom had accomplished his goal. His business ran effectively without his day-to-day involvement. Tom did not even need to be bothered signing checks. Only two people had access to the signature stamp: the bookkeeper and Tom's personal assistant. Tom's assistant would often run errands for him using her company American Express (AMEX) card. However, unbeknownst to Tom, his assistant was having financial problems at home. At first, she would sneak in a couple personal purchases while buying items for the company. Tom did not review the American Express statements in great detail, so he did not notice. Once she saw Tom was not watching closely, she got more aggressive with her purchases: groceries, a television, a down-payment on a car. She covered her tracks by intercepting the American Express statement the day it came in. She paid the bill in full using a company check and the signature stamp. Nothing seemed funny to the bookkeeper as AMEX was a valid vendor and the payment amounts were not completely out of line. Eventually, Tom realized he had not signed an AMEX check for a few months and was outraged to discover more than $20,000 in embezzled funds.

SOLUTION

You may not feel embezzlement can happen in your business, but I promise, it can. You typically have recourse against your bank if your signature is forged, but you most likely have no recourse if your employees use your signature stamp. Never use a signature stamp. You can have everything but the check signing done by someone else, but hand sign checks a couple of times a month. It will only take a few minutes, but signing your checks can save you thousands of dollars. Additionally, have your bank statements mailed to your home. Quickly review the charges and scan the physical checks. Something glaringly wrong, as in Tom's situation, can be quickly stopped.

Fatal Error #36:
You Snooze, Your Checks Bounce

The old axiom is true: you can only get money when you don't need it. You need to be taking premeditated steps to ensure your FUTURE credit needs, not today's needs.

REAL-LIFE EXAMPLE

Aaron's custom software business had been growing steadily for ten years. Every year was profitable. Aaron prided himself on his financial conservatism and stability. He had never laid off an employee, had cash reserves to pay six months of employee salaries, and saw no need for a line of credit when he had hundreds of thousands of dollars in the bank. Aaron's largest customer asked him to bid on a large piece of work that would effectively triple the size of Aaron's business, but after crunching numbers, Aaron realized he could not bid on the business because he could not fund the payroll until the receivables were collected. He scrambled to find alternative funding, but his long-time funding source, the Bank of Grandma, could not come through in time to submit the proposal.

SOLUTION

If you are fortunate enough to have strong financials, get a line of credit. If you don't, buddy up to your banker and hit them up when your financials turn to the good.

Get a small $100,000 line of credit, but only with no fees. A loan of this size will be based on your personal credit score, not your business creditworthiness. Use the line occasionally even if you don't need the funds and pay it back. This will show your bank that you can borrow money and pay it back. Ask for increases annually.

BONUS

This stinks, but banks tend to abuse you if there is no competition for your loan. This means filling out multiple loan applications, which is torturous. I suggest you visit *www.universalloanapplication. com* for ideas about how to easily apply for multiple bank loans. If you are shopping for a business loan without using the tools on this site, you are doing things the hard way.

NOTES:

_____

_____

_____

_____

_____

_____

_____

_____

_____

_____

Fatal Error #37:
Take Your Dramamine

It does not matter if yours is a service-oriented or a manufacturing operation, business comes in spurts. You will never be operating at 100% capacity all the time. Any business is much like a roller-coaster ride — there are dips and peaks. The ride is NEVER going to be flat, so take your Dramamine. What separates the men from the boys and the women from the girls is finding a way to raise the valleys NOT lower the peaks.

Your business should run smoothly AND profitably between 75% and 125% of capacity. If you are not capable of operating profitably within this range, there is a problem with your business model. For instance, many businesses slow down around Christmas or during the summer. Does your model include a plan for these slow times or do you complain about them every year?

REAL-LIFE EXAMPLE

John ran a custom software house. Inevitably, the projects all came at once and the business was feast or famine. John created a cash reserve of six months of payroll to cover the valleys, but this did not address the decline in profitability during the valleys. Additionally, John had a difficult time delivering projects on time during peak demand. John's way of addressing the problem centered on flexible outsourcing. He restructured the work to outsource some functions rather than entire jobs. Once functions could be delegated, he trimmed staff to 100% of capacity for the slow times, and he used outsourcing to cover the peak demand times.

SOLUTION

The following are some proven techniques to reduce the pain of business fluctuations:

1. Mandatory vacation windows. If you know you are going to be slow in the summer, force your employees to take one of their vacation weeks during the slow time. A variation of this strategy is a plant shutdown. Think of the havoc General Motors would have if they allowed all vacations when the employees requested them. The assembly line would always be running poorly. Instead, GM shuts down the line and orders everyone to take their vacation or lose it. Also, GM knows that they are going to lay out a ton of money with no production, and their financial plan takes this into account. This method is so much better than the small business method of enduring the pain all year long.

2. Make employees share the pain of business fluctuations. Business has changed quite a bit in the last 20 years. Employees have much more of a freelance mentality today compared to the "retire with a gold watch" days. You are making a mistake if you feel an obligation to lose money while maintaining your employees at 40 hours. Don't misunderstand me. If you have the financial luxury to do so, go for it — but most businesses don't. Sometimes, employees will gladly take the time off (unpaid) if you give them an opportunity. If they don't voluntarily take the time off, you may need to issue a mandate. Imagine the loss reduction that a 25% payroll reduction could create? If you manage your people well and the job you provide for them is truly a "good job," they will roll with the punches. Don't be afraid. However, if you have not done your part by creating a good job opportunity for them, your fears may be warranted. You very well may lose the employee if you reduce their hours. The problem is not the reduced hours, but the overall quality of the job.

3. Creative PTO. Check with your attorney, but you may have the option to "bank" some employee overtime and apply it during the bad times with paid time off options.

4. Find business opportunities that run contra to your primary business. Landscape companies plow snow. Public accounting firms aggressively bid governmental audits (their year-end is in the summer slow season). Manufacturers take in outside work during slow times. Software development companies place their employees on outside projects. **If you think hard enough, you can find something that will reduce the peaks and valleys.**

If you are in one of these cyclical businesses and have this issue, stop whining! There are two kinds of problems: ones that you are bigger than, and ones that are bigger than you. Don't let this problem be bigger than you!

NOTES:

_____

_____

_____

_____

_____

_____

Fatal Error #38:
Falling in Love with Your Inventory

Large businesses are terrible about having too little inventory. Smaller businesses are terrible about "falling in love with the inventory." First of all, at a fire sale, your inventory is probably only worth ten cents on the dollar, not the fifty cents your bank gives you on your borrowing base. Yes, there are exceptions. However, what would your inventory be worth if you had to get rid of ALL of it quickly. Yes, even the junk with the dust on it. For those readers who are in the service business, your inventory is labor, which is the most expensive inventory imaginable. You can't be too easy on yourself by saying inventory doesn't apply to you. You probably keep your "inventory" (staff) too long and cut back too slowly. Service "inventory" mistakes are far more costly than manufacturing ones. Labor is a very perishable commodity. A manufacturer can eventually sell their excess inventory — service companies can't.

REAL-LIFE EXAMPLE

Von was a used computer equipment dealer. The bulk of Von's profits were made buying used equipment for pennies on the dollar, warehousing it, and finding a client who still used the items. Von felt that too much inventory could not be an issue because he was buying it so inexpensively. However, Von's inventory consistently outgrew his ability to fund its growth through profits, so Von turned to a line of credit. The line grew too: $100K, $200K, $500K. Because Von acquired the inventory so inexpensively, he thought that controlling its cost seemed like a waste of time. Activities like physically inventorying all that stashed hardware on a regular basis seemed like a waste.

Here is the rub: Von finally did take a physical inventory. You know what happened next. All the newer models (valuable items) were short on inventory count. All the junk was over count. Von had let obsolescence and overstock go unchecked, and of the $650K of inventory on the books, only $250K was deemed sellable in the next six months. Von was forced into a "workout" situation with his bank, and it took him three years to recover. Von now carefully watches his inventory levels. Von says, "You are not collecting baseball cards. Inventory is only worthwhile if you can turn it into cash quickly."

SOLUTION

Be very cautious about adding inventory or staff. Find methods to run the company effectively while staff or inventory is lean. Stated the other way around: change your bias from too much staff/inventory to that of too little. Your "let's have it just in case" mentality is an expensive luxury, especially if the inventory is man-hours. Clean up your inventory once a year — get rid of the junk.

Fatal Error #39:
We Don't Need No Stinking Budget

Proper income and expense budgets are necessary to properly run a business, and operating without them is like driving blindfolded. Don't complain if you crash, Mr. Magoo. Some businesses may be so lucrative that the CEO can get away without proper financial controls, but good budgeting is part of good financial control and necessary for most businesses.

Some CEOs avoid a budget because they feel they are weak in accounting, but this is usually not true. A more accurate statement would be that they don't like accounting. Budgeting is not fun because it involves tough choices and sacrifice, but don't be confused. You will still have to make tough choices and sacrifice even without a budget. You will just be making choices unprepared and in a reactive fashion.

REAL-LIFE EXAMPLE

Kevin enjoyed a profitable business with net margins over ten percent, and sales had also been growing at around ten percent annually. Last year, however, sales took a nosedive and profitability turned to a loss. Kevin took a hard look at the expense side of the business and found that many categories of expense had "crept" up over the years, so much that Kevin found it difficult to rectify all of these expenses at once. Kevin also realized he had lost a good opportunity to "make hay while the sun was shining" by not tightly managing expenses earlier.

SOLUTION

Create and use budgets. If you truly are weak in accounting, get some training. One night class should be enough to sharpen your accounting skills to a point where they are not a liability. You can get assistance, but you cannot completely abdicate financial control of your business.

If you have and use budgets, kudos. However, I have seen many budgets that do not contain a miscellaneous category to cover the inevitable unexpected items that will occur over the course of the year. Miscellaneous expenses should include NO known expenditures, which should be categorized under "Other Expenses." Most companies budget ½ of one percent of sales to miscellaneous expenses. My guess is that you will miss your budget number if you don't have a miscellaneous expense line.

NOTES:

_____

_____

_____

_____

_____

_____

_____

_____

Fatal Error #40:
Flying Upside Down

For any CEO, managing objectively means quantifying every aspect of your business. Virtually everything can be quantified and measured, from quality to customer satisfaction. Some CEOs don't like to manage by the numbers because it takes away the gunslinger approach. Cold, hard numbers don't have the adrenaline rush of the daily gunfight. Not quantifying your business is the equivalent of flying a plane by feel. A good pilot uses a few key gauges in the instrument panel to fly safely. If any one of these gauges is out of whack, the pilot uses the other gauges to validate the reading and make the necessary adjustments. In fact, at high speed and altitude, fighter pilots cannot tell if they are upside down without the use of gauges. In the day-to-day battle known as business, you can easily get upside down without the use of your gauges.

The most important step to using gauges is creating key performance indicators (KPIs). These measurements are not limited to balance sheet and income statement items. These measurements drive and explain the financials. Theoretically, if the KPIs are "in line," the financial numbers will be in line. Let us look at the Ford Motor Company, to cite one example. Years ago they started rewarding employees for quality.[13] They gathered data on quality and compiled it into quantifiable terms. The concept was simple: if quality was in line, sales and profits would also be in line. Ford later became number one in truck sales because of these performance indicators.[14]

Consider the following key performance indicators:

---

13 Cascio, Wayne. *Managing Human Resources: Productivity, Quality of Work Life, Profits* (McGraw-Hill/Irwin; 7 edition, 2005)
14 Smith, L.R. Back to the Future at Ford, Quality Progress (USA), Mar 2005. Vol 38, No. 3: p. 50

- Dollars of product produced
- Utilization percentage
- Quality statistics
- Defect rate/return rate
- Dollars of sales per square foot
- Same store sales increase
- Inventory turns
- Sales funnel
- The number of salespeople employed. Buckman Labs (a 500 million dollar company) found that sales increased proportionately with each salesperson employed (after two years on the job — these were highly technical sales).[15]

REAL-LIFE EXAMPLE

Denise's manufacturing company had always been moderately profitable. Denise had always kept a close eye on sales figures and order-fill percentage since her factory produced hundreds of different parts. I convinced Denise to take a more creative view of the most critical measures. My view was that orders could not be shipped if product was not produced. Small batch, difficult-to-fill numbers could *not* be filled if the common parts were under-stocked because all available shop time was consumed producing the common parts. Both these issues could be most easily addressed by more efficient production. The more efficiently the common parts were produced, the more resources could be devoted to the time-consuming parts. Denise focused her attention on production efficiency. First, she started tracking units produced per man-hour, a measure that proved to have a better correlation to profits. Denise then tweaked the metric to measure dollars of product produced per man-hour, which proved to have the best correlation to profitability.

---

15 Peters, Tom. *Thriving on Chaos: Handbook for a Management Revolution* (New York: Alfred A. Knopf, 1987), pg. 173

SOLUTION

The bottom line does not magically appear. There are a few key indicators in every business that lead to a good bottom line. Find some key performance indicators and make them part of the way you run the business.

Using KPIs is like managing from a dashboard. It makes management more efficient and effective. Think of an airplane cockpit, which contains hundreds of instrument dials. However, the pilot only watches a handful of these dials. If everything is in line, none of the additional dials are relevant. If something is amiss on the main dials, the pilot digs deeper into the other instrument dials.

Create three to five KPIs. Monitor them daily, or weekly at a minimum. If you manage the KPIs well, your profitability will improve.

BONUS

Visit *51errors.com/kpi.html* for an extensive list of critical performance indicators.

NOTES:

_____

_____

_____

Fatal Error #41: Big Fish, Small Pond

Everyone wants their business to be as successful as possible, but even if your business's current performance far exceeds past performance, it may not be as successful as it could be. When you only trend against yourself, you are running a race against yourself. The only way to truly gauge your performance is to run the race against others by benchmarking against the best in the industry.

Benchmarking is the process of comparing your key performance indicators with other businesses in your industry. Although this is one of the few ways to establish best industry practices, few do it. Here are some examples of benchmarking data:

- Dollar of labor/unit
- Material COGS/unit
- Average utilization percentage
- Seasonal utilization percentage
- Net profit percentage
- COGS percentage
- Cost of freight
- Average worker salaries by position
- General & administrative costs as a percentage of total costs

REAL-LIFE EXAMPLE

Zach was troubled by the performance of his furniture store, and his assumption was that his salespeople were underperforming and overpaid. Zach always said, "If we could just do another one million dollars in sales, everything would be great." I challenged Zach to call a couple similar stores in faraway markets. Zach called some similar stores and found that they paid ½ the commission rate he paid. He also found their average salesperson sold three times more product annually. He found a nearly identically-situated store in Dallas that did almost double his sales, which proved to Zach that his ambitious sales target was not overly-ambitious. This discovery also caused Zach to take dramatic action regarding sales commissions. He lowered sales commissions from 10% to 7% effective immediately. Rather than quitting, the salespeople increased their sales to keep their income stable. Zach increased the net margins 3% immediately and continues to benchmark his critical measures with friendly competitors.

SOLUTION

I hear over and over again, "I want the benchmarking data, but none of my competitors will share it." If you want the data, there are ways to get it. You can simply ask your competitors for the information or you can use a third party to gather data if you are uncomfortable. Industry associations can help because associations often perform benchmarking studies (you may have to pay for this data in some cases). However, you might be surprised that your competitors want your data as much as you want theirs, but be prepared to sign a nondisclosure agreement. Be certain to emphasize that only those who share benchmarking data will have access to the results.

BONUS

Visit *51errors.com/mba.html* for more on benchmarking.

NOTES:

_____

_____

_____

_____

CHAPTER 5

Mule-Kicks

I have sprinkled Mule-kicks where appropriate throughout the book, but this entire section of the book is a Mule-kick, a big one, as it were. As a business coach, sometimes the best thing you can do for a client is kick them squarely in the butt to wake them up and get them moving (hopefully they do not fly across the table at me). I have used this technique for years and have seen Mule-kicks do wondrous things for my clients. A good Mule-kick can help you make millions of dollars.

You have three options to run your business. The first is to create a great business model, plan, create customers, etc. the best way you can. The emphasis in this option is on YOU. You run your businesses as yourself. That is, you start with a perfect business model to succeed in a diverse and varied world, including the marketing that will drive sales from a variety of customers. Then, YOU are plugged into this very objective, perfect world model with all your strengths and your weaknesses, all the things you like to do and the things you don't like to do, all your biases and your "way" of doing things.

Done right, however, you take your strengths and weaknesses into account BEFORE you design your model. Probably the best example of this is a business owner who hates sales. This owner should design a business model that does not require his or her input in the sales function. For instance, the business could rely heavily on marketing rather than selling.

However, this rarely happens. Instead, there is option two. The second method to run a business is to squeeze the square peg (the environmental variables) into the round hole (you). That is, the business is perfectly designed to work with the perfect CEO that can perfectly execute the large variety of duties. Technically, this is a bad business process. If we were creating a process to cook spaghetti, the process would be: buy or make noodles, fill a pan with water, boil the water, add noodles for 10 minutes, drain off the water by dumping the noodles into a strainer, return to the pan, add sauce, etc. Let's say you are the strainer in this example. However, you, the strainer, have no holes. The process looks great on paper, but when we apply you, the hole-less strainer, the process doesn't work well. In my opinion, this is the method by which most small businesses operate. This is not me saying, "You are stupid." This is me offering you another option to manage your business.

The third and best option is to **ACT** as CEO. That is, you must be the strainer WITH holes even though it is not your natural personality to be said strainer. Being a highly effective CEO involves moving outside your comfort zone. When you are saying or doing things you would not normally do as "you," what are you doing? Acting, right? The following errors are examples of instances when you may need to act outside your comfort zone. My two cents: suck it up. You will be a much better CEO if you can suck it up. At my company, we call sucking it up, "acting as CEO", and we call the necessary motivation in virtually any circumstance in which you must do something unpleasant, a Mule-kick.

Fatal Error #42:
Yabut

Yabut = yeah but... It is far easier to criticize someone else's work than to create something from scratch. Stop finding all the reasons an idea won't work and find a way to make it work. This is far more complicated than being positive vs. being negative. Yabut people always see why something cannot be done, whereas successful CEOs see the obstacles (YABUTs) and find the options to make an idea work in spite of them.

In addition to not engaging in this loathsome practice yourself, it is extremely important not to allow your people to YABUT. If you allow your people to explain why something will not work or get done, you are perpetuating a culture of non-performance.

Every CEO out there feels that their business culture is a performance culture. If you are tolerating YABUTs from yourself or your people, you DON'T have a performance culture.

REAL-LIFE EXAMPLE

Joe had spent the better part of six months crafting his marketing message. He created a structured sales process that had a more than reasonable opportunity to work. Everyone can guess what happened next. Not surprisingly, Joe's sales force did not have the degree of success expected. Instead of looking at their own selling skills or sales activities, Joe's sales force offered a host of complaints: we need better marketing, our price is too high, we need to add XYZ feature, and many more. What Joe's sales force was saying in realty was, "I can't sell this now, but I can sell this when..." As an outside observer, I determined that indeed Joe's marketing plan was good and should have worked. The problem was all the YABUTTING of the sales force. Every good sales manager knows that poor salespeople YABUT about better marketing. For those non-salesy types, "I can sell this better when the marketing gets better" is salesman-speak for "I can't sell Jack Squat!"

Fortunately, Joe recognized that the sales force was simply YABUTTING and stuck to his guns. He had to get rid of two salespeople. However, once he put a team of non-YABUTTERs in place, the sales came.

SOLUTION

First recognize if you are "YABUTTING." Then, if you see that you are allowing your people to YABUT, you have half of the problem solved.

Second, remove tasks/agenda items/priorities from your list. That's right, eliminate items. You will need this extra time to keep all your promises. You can't promise your people you will do something and then *not* do it. This sends a message to them that it is alright to promise something and not do it. This is the beginning of a negative business culture. Most CEOs try to do too much, but in attempting to do too much and failing, you send a message that YABUTTING is alright. It is all right to say NO! Saying that you are not going to tackle a project is much better than allowing it to fail or to stall out. These situations lead to "YABUTTING." By ridding yourself, as a leader, of the YABUTS, you are now ready to model, and to enforce, your standards with your employees.

BONUS

Visit *5lerrors.com/extras.html* to download a printable door sign to assist you in your battle against YABUTTERS.

NOTES:

_____

_____

_____

_____

_____

_____

_____

_____

Fatal Error #43:
Reinventing the Wheel Daily

I have asked thousands of business owners, "Who has an operations plan?" Ten percent of the hands go up. The next thing I say is, "Every hand in the room should have gone up! Everyone here is OPERATING, right? The people that raised their hands have a WRITTEN operations plan. Everyone else has one in their heads."

Every day a CEO with no written operation plan walks through the door, she says to herself, "Hey, I wonder how we should run the business today?" This process of reinventing the wheel will end up consuming all the valuable time of the organization and the CEO. In the name of flexibility and custom one-off solutions to problems, the CEO has doomed herself to a firefighting existence.

So, if writing an operations plan is so powerful, why don't 100% of businesses have one? Well, writing an operations plan is a REAL pain. It requires hard work, sacrifice, and a deep understanding of your business. Perhaps it is this deep understanding of the business that scares people away. If you do not have a full understanding of the business and its systems, you will be unable to write it, but nevertheless, don't let fear hold you back. The power of an operations plan is that you most likely do NOT understand your business systems at the beginning of the process, but you WILL understand them by the time you are done. This is the reason you do the plan. It is not the operations plan itself that is of value, but the process of doing it. Doing an operations plan will force you to refine and tighten your processes. It will also point out your "holes."

REAL-LIFE EXAMPLE

Prashant's business was driving him mad. He was making money, but nothing ever seemed to work unless he was personally involved. After a great deal of introspection, Prashant realized that his business was designed around people, not processes. People are not systems. People perform the systems. Prashant began crafting and implementing an operations plan. He started creating systems for the hiring and training of technicians. He figured that, if he could hire and train better technicians, many of the issues would disappear — he was right. He then tackled the customer service and sales process. Again, his personal involvement became less important for the business to execute well. As each system was added, Prashant gained time to focus on the big issues of the business: geographic expansion and profitability. Eventually, Prashant's business became wildly successful without his daily involvement.

SOLUTION

An operations plan is not something you want to tackle alone or you will most likely not finish it. There are no template programs to create an operations plan. The plan is custom to your business, so you cannot "borrow" someone else's and modify it. You have to start from scratch. Two ways to ensure you finish: hire a consultant to work with you, find a planning buddy in your business or another business owner who needs to write a plan, or create an accountability system for yourself such as a coach or mentor.

An operations plan primarily consists of the systems that run your business. The most common reason systems fail is the word "should." CEOs tend to write plans the way things "should" be done. Should is a VERY bad word in operational planning. How many things do your employees do the way they "should?" Don't answer; I already know. Believe it or not, I am not knocking your employees. They are simply human, and humans tend to take the path of least resistance.

Therefore, Rule #1 when creating systems is: **Work WITH laziness, not against it.**

Here are a couple of examples. First, remember when credit card readers first became available for pay at the pump? Did you ever pull up to the pump, realize it did not have a credit card reader, and then proceed to a gas station that did? I have. Have you ever waited in a drive-through line six cars long when you know there is no line inside? Have you ever driven around the mall parking lot over and over again when there are clearly open spots way at the back of the lot? These are all examples of how we don't behave logically, when we have not behaved how we "should."

I learned this lesson at my manufacturing company. Most of my factory workers were twenty-something slobs, and I could not stand how cluttered and messy the shop was (i.e., the SHOULD). So, I did what any logical CEO would do. I put a sign in the break room that said, "Your mother does not work here, so clean up after yourself." I bitched at them to clean up their workbenches daily. I set aside an hour-long plant shutdown every Friday solely for the purpose of housecleaning. Then, after implementing all my great ideas/systems, I nearly popped a gasket when I walked through the plant one afternoon and saw lunch sack after lunch sack simply thrown directly in the middle of the floor.

Instead of popping a blood vessel in my head, I decided to try something radically different. I tripled the number of trashcans in the shop. It was ridiculous. I made the decision that a trashcan should be no more than three strides away from any worker at any time. It WORKED! The shop was always tidy and I never had to say a word to anyone. I had found a way to make it easy for them to be clean, so they did so. This is how I learned to "work with laziness."

Most owners don't have the tenacity to write an operations plan, but an operations plan is a living breathing document that is never done. Therefore, starting and not finishing is no big deal precisely because you are never finished. I challenge you to spend a significant amount of time over the next year working on your operations plan. In one year, if you feel your time was not EXTREMELY well-spent, email me and I will extend $10,000 of products and/or services to you.[16]

BONUS

For detailed information on operations plans, visit *www.51errors.com/plans.html*

NOTES:

_____

_____

_____

_____

_____

_____

---

16 Certain conditions apply, see *51errors.com/opsplanchallenge.html* for details

Fatal Error #44:
A Pinch of This, a Pinch of That

If you fail to plan, you are planning to fail. But Jim, isn't this error the same as "My Cake is Flat"? Nope, this error is bigger because it involves not even having a plan or a recipe. You know who you are. You know the business. You have tons of experience. Blah, blah, blah. You STILL need a plan. The main reason people don't plan is that it seems like more work in an already hectic environment, but the biggest danger in failing to plan is that your activities will be incongruent. By this I mean that you will be working very hard but not accomplishing much. That is, you will be engaged in busy-ness without effectiveness. Many CEOs feel like they are on a treadmill, and they don't dare stop or slow down because they know they will be thrown from the treadmill. This is why creating a plan seems like more work they just can't afford to do.

However, if you fail to make your daily activities part of an overall plan, you are just perpetuating the cycle. To exit the treadmill, you must find a way to keep your current activities moving while moving forward on the truly "important" items.

REAL-LIFE EXAMPLE

Remember Ryce and her landscape company. She always seemed to be bogged down in the day-to-day details of the business. Ryce eventually began to feel like she was not making the progress she should, and after intense questioning, it became clear that Ryce understood the overall business dynamics as well as the future direction of the industry quite well. She foresaw the upcoming industry consolidation, and she could predict the shift in consumer preferences. Some of these industry "predictions" would dramatically change the business environment, and if the situation was handled well, her business could be catapulted to great heights. Handled poorly, these new dynamics could put her out of business. Fortunately, Ryce's failure to take the big picture into consideration and plan accordingly had not caused serious harm yet. However, if she continued on the same unaltered course for another two years, more organized competitors would have greatly diminished her business.

SOLUTION

Work the pyramid below. By this I mean, leverage your activities. The power of the pyramid is at the top, which is where vision and planning take place. The middle layer is where strategy takes place, and the bottom layer is where the daily activities occur. You are already engaged in some aspects of all of these. The problem is that they don't link together. Your daily activities can be mundane, but they MUST be part of a strategy, which in turn MUST be part of a vision or plan.

For example, if you have the vision to enter a new market, your strategy might be to purchase a competitor. The tactic might be to hire a business broker. The daily activity might be using your Rolodex to find broker candidates and calling them. If you do this, you can get off the treadmill.

BONUS

For a printable version of this diagram, visit *www.51errors.com/extras.html*.

NOTES:

_____

_____

_____

_____

_____

_____

_____

_____

_____

_____

Fatal Error #45:
Hogging the Information

CEOs tell me, "I need to clone myself because my people can't run things without me." You are right! They can't. Every CEO out there feels like their people don't make the same quality decisions they do. Right again. They don't. They don't have access to all the information you have. They also don't have the power to pull strings like you do.

Give your people the right to fail. Most CEOs reserve the right to fail for themselves, but without good information, you are setting your people up to fail. Things like basic objective financial data — margins, goals, etc. — can make an employee a better performer as well as give them the basic tools for good decision making.

REAL-LIFE EXAMPLE

Josh's rental business included hundreds of items, but unfortunately, customers also requested equipment Josh had to "borrow" from other vendors if he was out. This process seemed to be more art than science to Josh. Although Josh had many qualified staff who had been with the company ten years, he could not seem to get them to handle these special requests. When a customer called with one of these special requests, Josh had to drop everything, chase down competing vendors who would lend his company the equipment, and then determine how much to charge for these "specials."

Josh felt it was his 25 years of industry experience that made him the only one able to fill these special needs, but upon closer examination, Josh was hogging the information. Josh's problem was effectively solved by creating a spreadsheet with the following information: type of equipment, potential sources, average retail price, minimum and maximum margin targets. Of course, Josh also had to sacrifice the perfect solution to each request, his solution, for a reasonable solution provided by someone else.

SOLUTION

In reality, hogging the information makes YOU the culprit. Give your employees all of the data you have and see what happens. **If you do not have people who are trustworthy with this data, where does the fault lie?** If you give your employees an opportunity to succeed, you will see your business grow in unbelievable leaps and bounds, for these employees also have a stake in success.

Most CEOs, including me, have done something like this: Joe, your best salesman is going out on a million-dollar call. Everyone in the company is psyched. Joe comes back from the meeting and says, "Boss-man, this was the best sales call of my life. I did X and I did Y, and I came THIS close." Now, guess what I, the boss, would do? I'd go into my closet and pull out the cape and the outfit with the big S on the front. I'd go to the customer and play Superman. Sure enough, I would come back with the order. Joe says to me, "Wow Boss-man, I thought I was good, but you are da-bomb. How did you close them?" I say, "Well Joe, remember when I told you that you were fired if you sold below $37? Well, that price was a deal breaker so I sold for $36.80. And remember when I said our fastest delivery time was six weeks? Well, we have to get this one done in three weeks. And remember when I said extended warranties were killing margins? Well that was a deal breaker too, so I gave it to them."

You get the point. Did I "arm" Joe with the same tools and information that I had? No way! I had far different tools and data (like $37 really WASN'T the lowest price). What I have done is ask Joe to perform at the same level as I could but with far worse tools. I have created an unequal standard. My guess is that you are doing something similar.

NOTES:

_____

_____

_____

_____

_____

_____

_____

_____

_____

_____

_____

Fatal Error #46: Abdicating

W hen managers get lazy with delegation, they tend to abdicate. Abdication is not failure to delegate, but failure to *effectively* delegate. Abdication is washing your hands of the situation. Abdication is when you say, "I have had it up to here; you do it." Abdication has no training component, no follow-up component, and no feedback component. Abdication always fails unless the employee is a superstar with a long leash.

Conversely, delegation involves proper training and well-defined processes and procedures. However, most CEOs are far too busy running on the treadmill to create training or procedures, which forces them into abdication.

When abdication fails, CEOs fall into this trap: "I have to do everything myself." Now the cycle is complete. I call this "The Full Circle" (see the diagram below). The CEO has tried delegation, and it failed.

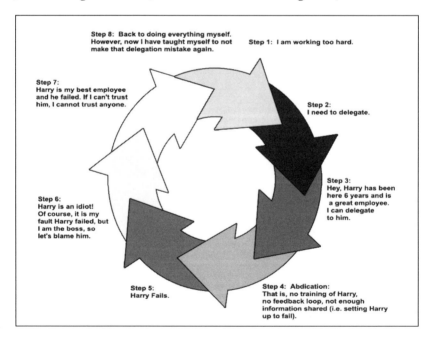

Step 8: Back to doing everything myself. However, now I have taught myself to not make that delegation mistake again.

Step 1: I am working too hard.

Step 2: I need to delegate.

Step 3: Hey, Harry has been here 6 years and is a great employee. I can delegate to him.

Step 4: Abdication: That is, no training of Harry, no feedback loop, not enough information shared (i.e. setting Harry up to fail).

Step 5: Harry Fails.

Step 6: Harry is an idiot! Of course, it is my fault Harry failed, but I am the boss, so let's blame him.

Step 7: Harry is my best employee and he failed. If I can't trust him, I cannot trust anyone.

Now they are stuck, trapped doing all the lower-level work that will NEVER drive the business forward.

REAL-LIFE EXAMPLE

Michael appeared to be an outstanding delegator. He possessed none of the mental blocks regarding trusting his employees. Michael was glad to remain out of the office for the biggest crises and "let his people handle it." In fact, Michael even passed my Christmas Ornament Test, which can reveal why most CEOs stink at delegation — they flinch. Picture this: An issue in your business is represented by a fragile glass Christmas ornament falling toward a hard floor. If it hits the floor, it will surely break into a million pieces. The business owner has lots of opportunities and the necessary information to spot problems much sooner than the employees do. Therefore, the CEO lunges for the ornament before his employees even recognize the problem (see the ornament falling). If the CEO had more trust in his people, better patience, or both, his people would most likely catch the ornament and save it from breaking. The problem is that most CEOs never give them that chance. We jump in too early and rob them of the opportunity to be of service to the organization.

Faililng the Ornament Test

To Michael's credit, his employees were decisive and trustworthy. However, six months later, Michael discovered that his bookkeeper's method of juggling tight funds included skipping the federal tax payments. Michael owed Uncle Sam $75,000. Michael's attitude of "you handle it" combined with no oversight at all led to this problem.

SOLUTION

You must break free of mental traps such as: the employees are not capable, it is too difficult, or the work will not be as good. This is head trash. These are YOUR issues. Give your people the proper tools, training, and leeway and they will NOT fail. You are failing them by not giving them the opportunity.

NOTES:

_____

_____

_____

_____

_____

_____

_____

_____

Fatal Error #47:
No Handbook

"I don't need a handbook; I have great people. I don't need a handbook; I have not had any problems." These are the excuses I hear. It only takes one problem to make a handbook well worth your effort. You are asking for lawsuits, behavior problems, and a bad business culture without a handbook. A common objection to creating a handbook is employee pushback. This is simply fear and not fact. There has not been an employee in the history of business that has quit over having a handbook.

REAL-LIFE EXAMPLE

Harry's manufacturing plant was hiring for the season, and Harry was excited with the interview of a particularly well-qualified candidate. During the interview, the manager told the prospective employee about the company's sick time and vacation pay, and after the employee was hired and worked a month, she asked for a day off and was granted paid leave for it. A week later, the employee was sick three days and was paid for her three days of sick leave. Two weeks later, the same employee had a family emergency and was given her full year's paid vacation. When Harry learned how much paid time off had been given to the employee, he sat her down and explained that he'd had enough. He also told her she had to "make up" the excess time she had been paid. The employee ended up quitting and collecting unemployment. Because there was no paid time off policy in place, this employee was paid far more than she was entitled. It could also be argued that the lack of a policy was a factor in her quitting.

SOLUTION

Why not seek out a good template for a handbook? There are many out there and they are not expensive. The project only takes a few hours. Remember what the payoff could be! Try *gneil.com* for sample templates.

BONUS

Visit *51errors.com/handbook.html* for free sample handbook templates.

NOTES:

_____

_____

_____

_____

_____

_____

_____

_____

_____

_____

_____

Fatal Error #48:
Reacting to the Sales Pipeline

Most businesses do not manage the upcoming business "pipe-line," but instead, look only at the closed business. This mismanagement leads to the ebb and flow problem, which is illustrated as follows:

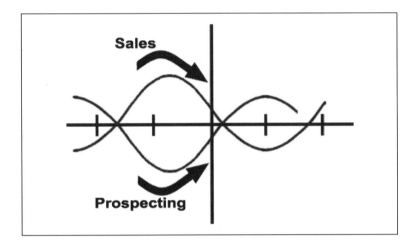

When sales are good, prospecting slows down; and when sales are bad, businesses scramble to sell. The problem with this approach is that it assumes sales can be closed quickly. However, most businesses have a sales cycle that takes three, six, or twelve months in which to close a deal. By the time they start to scramble, they have a three to twelve month period of lousy sales. These businesses have a tendency to "panic" and end up spending too much time in marketing or too much time in wasteful sales activity.

REAL-LIFE EXAMPLE

Lin-Wang had a successful consulting business. Indeed, it was too successful at times. Lin-Wang was so busy trying to find consultants for current client engagements that he had to cancel all those "non-productive" activities: visiting clients/prospects, golf and marketing activities. Lin-Wang was swimming in cash from all the work, but nine months later, Lin-Wang started to sense a slow-down. It seemed like all the jobs were coming to an end around the same time. Lin-Wang began to look at the upcoming projects, but there were far too few to keep even half the staff busy, and he began aggressively prospecting and marketing, but his strategy was too little and too late. The sales cycle was far longer than Lin-Wang had to market, and he was forced to have a massive layoff and risked losing some excellent talent.

SOLUTION

Successful selling is always a proactive activity, not a reactive one. Failing to manage your pipeline puts you in a "reactive" mode. Create a funnel or pipeline model that fits your business, and use this pipeline to manage your sales and your salespeople. **Theoretically, if your pipeline model is accurate, and you manage the pipeline well, you will never have a revenue surprise.**

BONUS

For sample sales pipeline models, visit *www.51errors.com/sales.html.*

NOTES:

_____

_____

_____

_____

Fatal Error #49:
Under-Managing the Sales Force

Many CEOs feel that they don't fully understand the sales process, and consequently, they don't manage it. They say things like, "Don't just stand there, sell something." Guess how many times this works? **NONE!** You do not need to be a sales expert to manage the sales process.

If you don't believe me, watch Alec Baldwin play a hard-nosed sales manager in *Glengarry Glen Ross*. My suspicion is that Alec Baldwin, the actor, has never managed a sales force, but you would never know that by his performance. Go to *youtube.com* and search for "Glengarry Glen Ross speech." Play the longest version. It just keeps getting funnier.

Sales is like any other function of a business: there are inputs and outputs. Those inputs and outputs are either acceptable or unacceptable. The difference between the CEOs who are "strong" in sales and those who are not is nothing more than this simple secret: the strong sales CEOs don't put up with BS from the salespeople, whereas the weaker sales CEOs know that they don't know how to get sales and so are at the mercy of the sales force. They give the sales force a ton of slack. Most salespeople are not good folks to be given excess slack.

REAL-LIFE EXAMPLE

April was an ex-Big 5 accountant, and she was a strong operational leader for her business. She also viewed salespeople as unscrupulous, annoying and lazy. April was savvy enough to realize she needed salespeople, but she wanted as little to do with them as possible. April's three salespeople produced decent results, and the company grew 15% annually for years. Profitability was good.

I challenged April to monitor and manage sales a bit, and her results were impressive. By better managing the sales pipeline and rescuing a few sales (based upon pre-determined criteria), April was able to push annual growth to 22%.

SOLUTION

The bulk of the sales management problem occurs at the beginning of the process, that is, keeping crummy salespeople on the payroll. You cannot be afraid to fire bad salespeople. Losing a salesperson who isn't selling much only saves payroll, and you should remember that only one in ten salespeople is a true superstar. Therefore, you may have to fire nine to find the one superstar, and you must create an objective system to find out if a salesperson is a dud very early in the employment relationship. You should be able to create a system with a 30/60/90-day plan. This plan should be objective enough so that the salesperson can tell you if they have been successful, but it is possible that this measurement system may not be centered on closed sales. This is a common problem. Poor sales managers feel that the only way to gauge salespeople is through closed sales, but there are many, many other ways to measure a salesperson's success. I have created a process called SalesMapping that fixes many common sales management issues.

BONUS

Visit *mysalesmap.com* to learn about creating a SalesMap for your company. My clients have used SalesMapping for many years with incredible results.

Fatal Error #50:
Playing the Blame Game

If you have said any of the following, you have played the "Blame Game":

- Why won't they just do as I say?
- Why can't I find any good employees?
- What does it take to get people to complete tasks within the assigned timeframe?
- My stupid competitors are lowering prices again.
- The government is over-regulating our industry.

Being a CEO is the toughest job in the world because the buck always stops with you. Directly or indirectly, **EVERYTHING** is your fault because you are in control of every aspect of your business even if you are pretending that you are not in control of it.

REAL-LIFE EXAMPLE

Ivan owned a jewelry store. One day when I walked in, he screamed, "Why can't I just get people to do what I say? Sometimes, my employees are just stupid." After letting him rant for a while, I asked some tough questions: Who hired them? (Ivan.) Who trained them? (Ivan, if anyone.) Why do they still work here if they are so stupid? (Because Ivan had not fired them.)

Eventually, I convinced Ivan that the problems were HIS problems and completely within his control. Ivan stopped complaining and started acting. It took some time for all the problems to be solved, but at least his blood pressure dropped considerably.

SOLUTION

I have a little rule: You can't control how an employee behaves or the specifics of what they do — you can only control the environment they operate in. Translation: you have no idea whether your employees are going to behave the way you want. You can only set up an environment that ENCOURAGES or DISCOURAGES them to do what you want. The examples are many. For instance, let's say tardiness drives you insane. You could create a policy that says, if an employee has more than one tardy in a month, they are fired. My guess is that tardiness would drop dramatically. We will ignore the other fallout from this policy such as having to pay more, massive firings monthly, etc. However, such a policy does create an environment where tardiness would be virtually non-existent. The Pike Place Fish Market in Seattle was made famous by the book *Fish Stories.* The fish market has a reputation as a great place to work. Let's say a Grumpy Gus-type guy went to work there. My guess is that he would quit or "snap into line" and be more "fun." This is the power of corporate culture, of the work-environment you create. Focus your time and energy on creating an optimized environment, not bitching about your employees' dumb behaviors.

Who is to blame is the wrong question. Why this happened is the right question. What is wrong with your systems that caused the problem? Fix the systems and you will fix the problem. Put different people into the same bad system, and the new people will fail as well. Ultimately, you are the CEO; it is ALL your fault, not theirs. Fire them if they are not competent. Fix the systems. Worry about the why, not the who.

NOTES:

_____

_____

_____

_____

_____

_____

_____

_____

_____

_____

_____

Fatal Error #51:
Know What to Do, Just Don't Do It

Entrepreneurs are generally a pretty bright group, so why don't they do the right things? The main reason is that they are out of "attention units." There are only so many things upon which you can focus your attention. Consider a plate of food that is full. If you put more food on it, different food just falls off. Have you ever felt like your brain was "full," that the next thing you needed to remember would automatically push something out of your mental "files"? This is being out of attention units. My guess is that you ARE out of attention units. Therefore, when you try to "do the big stuff" that you "should" be doing, you simply can't.

Also, because CEOs often do not have bosses or boards of directors, they lack accountability. So many times their shortcoming has nothing to do with "wrong ideas," but rather, their shortcoming stems from not executing the ideas they already have.

REAL-LIFE EXAMPLE

Holly had owned her travel agency for thirty years. When the travel industry started to feel pressure from the Internet, Holly cut expenses and doubled her sales efforts. A few years later, the terror attacks took another bite out of her business. Holly watched travel agencies going broke left and right. When Holly was asked how she could survive in the age of the Internet, she said, "I can't." Holly knew her business was doomed in its current form, but she kept forging ahead unchanged.

SOLUTION

Trust your intuition. The experts tell us that our intuition is never wrong, only our interpretation of that intuition. I had a client in a terrible business situation. He simply needed to exit the business before it killed him. He was having chest pains every Sunday evening before the upcoming week began. Everyone around him was telling him to jump ship, but he simply refused to hear their warnings. His determination and drive would not let him accept the obvious solution. Being a CEO necessitates decisive, and sometimes painful, action.

Another big complaint I hear is, "I know what I need to be doing, but I just don't have the time to get around to it." Putting the time into your highest impact activities is akin to "paying yourself first." When you follow the "get around to it" approach, you guarantee that all the little, meaningless tasks (the crap) GET done and that the big, meaningful, impactful stuff DOESN'T get done.

NOTES:

_____

_____

_____

_____

_____

_____

_____

_____

_____

NOTES:

Now What?

You have read all 51 Fatal Errors, but now what? First and foremost, let's focus on ACTIONS, not on thoughts or theories. One of the knocks we hear from business owners about the popular business press is "great ideas, now what?" All the great ideas in the world will not make your business more valuable. Only those ideas that you successfully implement will make your business grow.

One of the goals of this book is to get you energized about making positive changes in your business, but we need to temper this enthusiasm with some realism. Your calendar is most likely full. Your time is limited for making sweeping changes. **Baby-steps, which are actually implemented, are far more powerful than sweeping changes that stay on the drawing board.**

Another danger is what I call the "with a twist" syndrome. You are making changes but the changes simply aren't dramatic enough. You had iced tea before, and now you order some iced tea with a twist of lemon. So what? You can do better than "with a twist."

The following is a step-by-step action plan to improving your management and your business:

Phase One:
Work on Building Your New C.E.O.

Unfortunately, you are always the bottleneck of your business. The good news is that improving your personal effectiveness will directly result in a more productive business. Let's start by getting rid of the emotional baggage. We all have far too many "incompletes" in our lives. Make a list of everything you have been meaning to do or that is half-done. Eliminate a big chunk of it. That's right: just say no to some of it! Now finish some the items to which you are unwilling to say no. You will know when to stop because you will feel some sense of relief. This sense of relief is also a source of energy. You will use this energy to accomplish additional objectives.

Our next step is to eliminate your low-impact activities and move your Delegation Line. Don't take this as a "knock." Even Jack Welch has high-impact and low-impact activities. Keep a time log for one week. Create no more than ten categories and categorize each fifteen minute period of your day. Make sure you have a category for "inefficiency or lost time." On Saturday, review where you are spending your time. You will most likely be surprised how much of your time is spent on day-to-day items that do not drive long-term value for your business.

Now, you need to figure out how to delegate or eliminate these low-impact tasks. Ideally, you should delegate the function, not the task. When you delegate the task, you keep the responsibility, which only gets rid of part of the work. Your goal should be to offload one third to one half of your day-to-day work.

One of the pitfalls of delegation is that you have to be willing to "buy back your own time." If you do the accounting work yourself, it is "free." If you pay someone, you spend cash. Many entrepreneurs are unwilling to buy back their time. You are wearing the Dog Collar when you can't get rid of it. You must have confidence in yourself that you can make yourself more valuable than the cost of buying your time back. You may not be able to see how it can financially work today, but you CAN do it!

If you are ambitious, you can increase your personal productivity further by reading and implementing David Allen's book, *Getting Things Done*.[17] His book is outstanding because it is very tactical rather than theoretical.

Phase Two: Learn How to Act

Like it or not, management is acting. You are not the real you at work; you are playing a role as the manager of your business. Why not play the role of the BEST manager of your business? If Jack Welch or some other "super-manager" came in to run your business, what would he do differently? Seriously, write it down, now!

_____

_____

_____

_____

_____

Why can't you do the same? You can! Learn to play the role of benevolent dictator. It's just an act. It is not the real you. Be more decisive. CEOs are paid to make decisions. Gather all the data quickly, then take action. Mistakes will be made, but so what if you are wrong? Some

---

17 Allen, David. *Getting Things Done: The Art of Stress-Free Productivity* (Penguin Books, 2003)

of the world's great successes arose from failures. The Macintosh was born from the failed Lisa computer. The wildly successful 1965 Ford Mustang had many parts and designs borrowed from the not-so successful Ford Fairland and Ford Falcon. Toys R Us arose from the ashes of a failed department store chain. Microsoft DOS was originally a partially-working version of another company's operating system. To take your business acting to the next level, visit *www.actingasceo.com* for ideas.

Phase Three: Hire Better

Most CEOs hire based upon an employee's resume and their ability to talk well during an interview. Both of these characteristics are not particularly useful on the job. Instead, create a testing system that closely emulates the actual job. Create an assembly test for factory workers. Use online computer skills testing for office workers. Have a salesperson make fifty cold calls in front of you.

The key word is **aptitude.** Aptitude cannot be discovered from a resume or interview. Aptitude is the ability to learn a skill quickly. Employees with a high degree of aptitude will always perform better. Find out what your current key employees' aptitudes are and find a test. Then use this test to screen new hires. Forget the resumes. Make your own test if needed.

Phase Four: Train Better

Training high-aptitude employees is easier than expecting the employees you hire for their interview skills to perform well once hired, but excellent training systems are still needed. One of the stumbling blocks for proper training is impatience. Typically, we need a contribution from new hires immediately, so we don't have the luxury of the time to train. This time constraint could create a recipe for failure.

Here is a simple training concept that is very counter-intuitive: it is better to have an employee who can master a very small task than an employee who can do a small portion of a large volume of tasks. The employee who can master ANYTHING is HELPING! The employee who has nothing mastered needs constant help and is IN THE WAY. You don't have time to help, and this employee is doomed to fail.

Break the training into tiny steps, eliminating as much variety as possible. Variety kills training. For new hires, make the exceptions to the procedures non-existent — Don't even tell them about the exceptions until they have mastered the basics. A good training system is like building a house out of bricks. Each mastered skill is a brick in the wall. Eventually, a house will be built. Throwing too many items at a new employee is like dumping all the bricks in an unsturdy pile and calling it a house.

Phase Five: Create Systems

As you know, the systems are more important than the people running them. As a side benefit, once you create the systems that run your business, these systems become YOUR intellectual property. In fact, EVERYONE is in the intellectual property (IP) business whether they know it or not.

You think you are in the IT staffing business? Really? How do you add value? My guess is that you have the systems and the know-how that allow you to recruit and train needed IT staff so that customers will pay you more for their staffing needs than it costs you to provide those needs. Isn't that intellectual property? Doesn't that make your "real" business a knowledge business?

Okay, keep going? How about a tough one, manufacturing. Is a widget manufacturer in the business of making stuff? No! The manufacturer of widgets has processes that they perform better than the competition. We call this "competitive advantage." Where does competitive advantage arise from? Doing something better than the competition, right? Isn't that IP? If you have a vendor you buy from that is cheaper/better, isn't that IP? In short, if you have a process that allows you to train better people or hire better people — that is competitive advantage and that is IP. If you can manufacture a product more efficiently with better machinery, that is still IP. The IP is knowing what machine to own, how to use it, etc.

If the intellectual property at your company resides with the person performing the task, you have little or no intellectual property in **your own systems.** This is unacceptable! If the employee leaves, the system and the IP leaves.

Flowcharts are a great place to start with systems. There is no need to get overly complicated. Keep it simple. Ignore the anomalies. Surprisingly, most systems fail when CEOs insist on dealing with every anomaly because they overcomplicate the task and make it seem overwhelming. Have your people come to you if there is an anomaly. You will have worked yourself out of much of the daily grind, so dealing with an anomaly or two will not kill you.

Be willing to "put your stake in the ground." That is, pick a specific, objective solution DESPITE its imperfections and STICK WITH IT. Recognize that not all solutions will be perfect. A subjective solution, one provided by you for each specific situation, will ALWAYS be better than a generic solution, but a subjective solution requires YOU, your input. An objective and somewhat imperfect solution does not require your input and is an excellent tradeoff. Once you have the basic flowchart, you can formalize it in a program like Microsoft Visio, which allows items to be easily moved around a flowchart.

Now, turn your flowchart into a training system, but remember that people rarely read, and frequently misunderstand, words. A picture is truly worth a thousand words, and video, a series of pictures, is a simple and easy way to train employees. The great aspect of video training is that you create a training library, and you need to do the training only once. If you would like examples of sample training systems, you can visit *www.51errors.com/systems.html.*

Phase Six: ENJOY

R unning a business is supposed to be the best job in the world, and you are supposed to enjoy it. **Remember, it is your business's function to serve YOU, not the other way around.**

I sincerely hope you have found this book useful and thought provoking. Thank you for taking the time to read and to digest its contents, and I welcome your comments. I can be reached at *author@51errors.com.*

NOTES:

_____

_____

_____

_____

_____

_____

The 51 Fatal Business Errors Programs

If you are looking to jumpstart your implementation of the lessons learned in the *51 Fatal Business Errors*, we offer several options to accelerate your business growth:

51 Errors Coaching Club
www.ceocoachingclub.com

What is it?

- Each week, you will receive a summarized Fatal Error with updated commentary from the author of 51 Errors himself... Jim Muehlhausen!
  — Delivered via your choice of video/audio postcard/mp3/ podcast
- **Greatest Hits** coaching series delivered monthly
  — The most important business lessons filtered from 2500+ live sessions into a 45 minute audio session
  — This product allows you many of the benefits of live coaching for a fraction of the cost. Each month, we pull knowledge from our nationwide coaching network and condense it into 45 minutes of fast-paced learning. Every month, you receive:
    ~ A fast-paced session on an essential business topic in Mule-kick style. A straightforward, no B.S. how-to so you can improve your business. This session can be played in your car, on your computer or on an IPod
    ~ A worksheet to reinforce the coaching session and give you next action steps
    ~ An outline of the coaching session for easy review
    ~ A review of a top business book with the "need to know" information minus all the fluff

~ Supplemental session for added learning and additional action items. This section also includes:

  - New business trends you need to know to keep your market edge
  - A new management technique you must employ
  - The best of the best-practices from businesses around the country
  - A cost-saving trick that will blow your socks off
  - A fancy MBA-type trick that you can actually use
  - A personal and business coaching topic of the month. Examples include:
    • Turbo-charging your personal productivity
    • How to set meaningful goals and training yourself to hit them EVERY time
    • How to systematize your business to create maximum value and income
    • Creating a training and hiring system that is simply unbeatable
    • Getting the most from your employees: the theoretical and the practical
    • Creating critical performance measures: a key to driving maximum profitability
    • Creating profitable work/home balance

• Access to our monthly business brainstorming call. Each month, business owners from around the country join us to brainstorm and share best practices on a specific issue:
  — Example topics:
    ~ Increasing margins
    ~ New business ventures
    ~ Retaining key employees without paying too much
    ~ Attracting top talent away from bigger companies

- ~ Creating a can-do company culture
- ~ Outsourcing functions to India/China/Philippines without going insane
- ~ Selling your business for top-dollar instead of just bailing out

Coaching Club Bonuses

Each coaching club member receives:

- 1 year free use of faqdesigner.com ($119 value)
- "Acting as CEO video" ($99 value)
  - — Learn how Hollywood secrets can greatly improve your management abilities
- 6 Power Exercises to get the most from your people ($79 value)
- 3 months free membership in The 51 Errors Inner Circle ($237 value)
  - — Jim Muehlhausen hosts a 2-hour call where you can bring your most important business issues
  - — Calls are recorded so you can access them for later playback

How much does it cost?

$49.95/month billed to your credit card or Paypal

Learn more at www.ceocoachingclub.com

How long is the contract?

There is no contract. If you don't like the service or simply aren't using it, simply drop us an email and you're done

Seems too cheap?

You're right. This is a ton of value for the money. My goal is to become a trusted source of business information to you. If I need to offer a great deal to get you started, so be it. Once you see the value of my products, my guess is that you will want more

THE 51 FATAL BUSINESS ERRORS — AND HOW TO AVOID THEM

Nine week tele-class

- FREE session for all book purchasers (go to *www.51errors.com/ free.html*)
- Led live by the author
- Includes 51 Errors workbook, study guides, checklists, and action guides for each module
- Students will learn:
  - Specific action steps necessary to eliminate all 51 errors
  - Specific action steps to move past the errors and make their company world-class
  - How to effectively coach their staff around the 51 errors
  - Learn to become a Green Collar CEO
- Who should attend?
  - Anyone who wants to quickly improve their business and their bottom line
  - Anyone who prefers a structured program vs. a do-it-yourself approach
  - Anyone who wants access to the author for specific questions and assistance
- Specifics
  - For dates and times, visit *www.51errorsworkshop.com*
  - Individual modules $129, entire course $499
  - Cost $499 for the 1st attendee, $249 for each additional attendee

Week-long intensive 51 Errors workshop

- Visit *www.51errorsworkhop.com* for details
- Held annually in Chicago or Dallas
- $2,995 per attendee

Audio Book

- If you prefer audio books, please visit *www.51fatalerrors.com* or amazon.com to purchase the audio version of the book.

Affiliates

- If you know business people who could benefit from the 51 Errors program, check out or affiliate program at *www.51errors.com/affiliate.html.*

51 Errors Certified Coach

- Want to teach others the lessons in the 51 Errors? Learn how to become a certified 51 Errors coach at *www.51errors.com/coach.html.*

Reference Table: Plain English Titles